Passing Life's Little Tests (My Life Before and After Parkinson's Disease)

April Allen Poe

April Allen Poe

Acknowledgements

I'M HAVING A hard time remembering just how many people helped make this book happen. Of course, I want to thank my mom who has always encouraged me and believed in me no matter what the project.

And the list of friends to thank is large. I can't possibly list everyone, but will give special thanks to Ellen and Margo, who you will get to know when reading this book. Thanks also to my co-worker, Mandi, who read my stories and always responded in a way that helped me believe I had stories worth telling.

Thanks to Anna who volunteered to edit my book more than once even though we barely knew each other.

Each person in these stories deserves thanks because the stories would not exist without them, friends and strangers alike.

April Allen Poe

Introduction

THIS IS A book about some not so average things happening to an average person (me). I'm sure everyone has funny stories to tell about unusual things happening to them. But recently, when I've told these stories, people have said "you should write a book," so I did write a book. I hope you enjoy it and that maybe it will make you recall funny events from your life.

When you pick up a book, do you ever ask "what can I possibly get out of this book that might benefit me?" My hope is that I make you laugh and consider how a sense of humor can help you pass life's little tests so that you are more able to deal with the inevitable larger tests we all face. Secondly, I hope that you will be reminded of the power of words to change lives.

As I was writing these stories, I continued to learn things about myself and life in general. A few of these lessons are:

1. Life will continue to test us and our most powerful weapons are a strong sense of humor and the ability to see the positive in a negative situation.
2. Each of these lessons helped me become the strong person I am today.

Names have been changed to provide privacy.

Table of Contents

Part 1

Opening Story

Our Realtor

THIS STORY IS one I like to tell in person because of the look on the faces of my friends when I tell it. What I see on those faces is complete disbelief. I know they think I'm making it up, but I promise it is the truth. This is the story that got me writing in the first place.

I met my husband when I was almost 40 and we both owned houses. When we decided to get married, we planned to sell my house first while living in his house, then we could sell his house when we found one that was new to both of us.

We wanted to try selling it ourselves so that we put some extra money in our pockets, not a realtor's pocket. But we didn't have much luck selling it ourselves. We felt lucky when we found a realtor who would give us a discount on his fee since we were doing some of the work. After about a month of showing the house, we got an offer which turned into a sale, and we had a closing scheduled. The realtor sign was still in the front yard. This fact will become more important shortly.

We were staying at my house and I was reading the local newspaper on a Sunday morning. I began reading an article about a bank in a nearby suburb that had been robbed and the accused man had the same name as our realtor. I pointed that out to my husband and he said there was no way it was the same person. I just felt in my gut that it was the same person. I looked in our local phone book and there was only one listing for that name. I still believed it was our realtor but my husband kept saying "no way."

About an hour later someone knocked on the door. When I answered the door, there was a man with his arm extended towards me and he handed me his business card which had the name of a realty group on it, along with his name. Then he said "I thought you might be looking for a new realtor since yours is in jail for robbing a bank." This man had seen the sign in the yard and thought it would be a good lead for him. Part of me wanted to laugh because the whole thing was a riot. And another part of me wanted to celebrate the fact that I was right about it being our realtor who robbed a bank. Robbed a bank?!? What would motivate someone to rob a bank? And do they really think they will get away with it? Apparently, he even used his mentally challenged sister to drive the getaway car. But we did get to our closing and his mother represented us. Not surprisingly, she never mentioned the robbery.

Early Childhood

Thumb Tack Safety

WHEN I WAS very young, maybe 4 or 5, we lived in a two-story house. My bedroom was on the second floor. We were having a particularly hot summer and had no air conditioning. My mom decided to put a fan in the window to help keep me cool. She was very cautious and put a screen in front of the fan to keep my little fingers safe. She used thumb tacks to keep the screen between me and the fan. She believed in safety first.

Apparently, I fell out of bed during the night and cried out for my mom. She came and comforted me and put me back in bed. I got up the next morning and everything seemed fine until my mom combed my hair and the comb got stuck on the tack stuck in my head. Afraid of hurting me, my mom took me to the local emergency room. The doctors had never seen such a thing. They had to create a special tool to remove the tack. I was the talk of the hospital that day.

Donkeys – Not My Friend

WE ARE TAUGHT as children that we can always trust our parents, because as parents, their job is to keep us from harm. I believed this was true until I learned the hard way, at the ripe old age of about 10, that it is even more important to trust the little voice in our heads.

I grew up in a suburb of Dayton, Ohio, and it was in an era when it still had a small town, homey feel, a time when no one considered that leaving your doors unlocked could be dangerous. At Christmas time, different organizations would sponsor a live nativity scene, with Mary, Joseph, baby Jesus and various live animals. One of these animals was a donkey.

Our whole family made a special trip to this nativity scene, mostly to see the animals. There was a wooden fence all around to keep the animals where they belonged, but many kids my age were standing on the fence and reaching over to pet the animals. I wasn't interested in petting them, not after seeing the donkey's giant teeth. But my dad, my trustworthy dad, told me to go ahead and pet the donkey, that he wouldn't hurt me. I said no, thank you. I really didn't want to have anything to do with the donkey, but my dad really wanted me to pet the donkey. So, just to put this dialogue to rest, I reached over the fence to pet the donkey and guess what...the donkey bit me. Those great big chompers I was trying to avoid, came together on my arm, which did not make me happy. The only thing that kept me from harm was the fact that I was wearing a heavy coat. Even with the coat, there were distinct teeth marks on my arm. Even now, I can't say that I have any great love for donkeys.

Brave Dad

WHEN I WAS around 11 years old, I had hurt my knee doing something really stupid. There was a dead end street near our house that about 10 houses on it, so there was very little traffic, which made it a great place to play. One day I felt extra brave and came up with something I thought would be lots of fun. I put on my roller skates and tied a rope to the back of my friend's bike. While I held onto the other end of the rope, my friend pedaled with all her might, pulling me up and down the street. But, you know, sometimes when you are having fun, it is easy to get wrapped up in the moment and not notice something important. Well, that happened to me. There was one relatively small pothole in the road that I had successfully rolled around several times without a problem. Then I got careless. I hit that hole with my skate which made me fall. I then dropped the rope which somehow got tangled in one of my skates, and my friend dragged me for what seemed a long time. I'm sure it was probably only seconds, but felt much longer from where I was. I stood up and brushed myself off and walked home to show my mom my wounds. When it was all said and done, I had a broken elbow and had damaged my knee.

As a part of the treatment for my damaged knee, I had to go to the local hospital and get a cortisone shot in my knee about every six weeks. I'll bet those of you who have gotten cortisone injections are grimacing, right? After each shot, I would be on crutches for a couple of days, then the pain would be less and I could get around fairly normally. My mom had always taken me to my appointments, but one day she wasn't able to take me, so my dad took me.

I had gotten multiple shots by this time and knew what to expect, but this was all new to my dad. He drove me to the hospital and we got into a room pretty quickly. There was a new nurse working that day, one I had not seen before. She came in and talked to me, explaining what I should expect. Then she asked me if I would prefer lying down when I got the shot and I said no. Dad asked why I might want to lie down and the nurse explained that it was a very painful procedure and that some people faint from the pain. Then my dad kind of lost it, saying "What do you mean she might pass out? Why couldn't you make it less painful?", or something to that effect. Then I got my shot, without passing out, and he wanted to carry me out of the hospital instead of me using crutches like usual. At 11 years old, I could not think of anything more embarrassing! He finally let me use the crutches, but I think he never got more than 6 inches away from me, I guess to make sure he was close enough to me that he could rescue me should I start to fall. I look back now and understand that he was just trying to protect me from harm, which I guess is a dad's primary job.

Glass Doors

WE LIVED IN a suburb that was a mix of ranch houses and 2-story houses. The ranch houses all had a glass sliding door at the back of the garage, and a lot of families converted their garage into a family room, which made the glass doors perfect for that space. My brother had a friend who lived in a ranch house where the garage was not converted and was empty much of the time. Their driveway sloped down from the garage and was pretty steep. And on this particular day, these facts lead the boys to a new adventure.

It was the middle of the winter and we had had an ice storm which made the driveways and the yards very slick, much like a skating rink. These daredevil boys came up with a daring plan. They opened the front garage door and then opened the back sliding glass door. They got out a garden house and sprayed down the floor in the garage. They waited a while until that water became ice and linked the driveway to the garage floor and the garage floor to the back yard, all of which were now icy.

Then, one by one, a boy would start at the very far side of the back yard and run until they got some momentum and then let themselves slide on the ice through the garage and down the driveway. They each had a couple of turns and it was now my brother's turn again. So he started running, and was in slide mode when the boy's mother came out of the house and into the garage. She saw that the glass door was open, so she shut it. This all happened so quickly that my brother wasn't able to stop in time, and went through the glass door. He did have time to put his hands up to cover his face. My brother was actually very lucky that day. If he had not covered his face and had not been wearing layers of winter clothes, he would have been more seriously hurt. He did have to have quite a few stitches but he healed quickly and promised never to do that again.

The Teen Years

History in the Making

IN THE LATE 1960's, it wasn't unusual for young people to protest the Vietnam War. I was too young to be a part of it, but not too young to witness it.

My grandparents owned a restaurant/grocery store at Indian Lake in Ohio, which was a small resort sort of town. Its most popular attraction, besides the lake, was an amusement park on the lake. In those days, my mom felt comfortable letting me and my brother, ages 12 and 13, go to the amusement park alone. Going to the amusement park was one of my happiest childhood memories. That is, until the protesters showed up.

One weekend in particular, the protesters were especially visible. We were at my grandparents' restaurant and we could see a group of young people (protesters) being walked down the main road that led out of town. The protesters were walking ahead of the police. Then we saw the police walking alone in the opposite direction, heading back towards the amusement park. Then we would wait a little while and we would see the protesters return to the park. The next thing you know, we would see police directing the protesters out of town again. This happened several times and I imagine the police were getting tired of the game.

At one point, the police must have felt the protesters were getting unruly because they threw a tear gas canister at someone. And, unfortunately, that someone was standing in front of the restaurant which had a screen door. Without warning, the restaurant was filled with tear gas. Take my word for it, you don't ever want to be anywhere near tear gas. It was so bad that my grandparents didn't ask any of the patrons to pay for their meals. We didn't know it at the time, but we had just witnessed a part of history. Mention the 1960's and most people think of Vietnam or Woodstock. I remember the tear gas!

Ugly Glasses

I'VE WORN GLASSES since I was 11 years old, and probably needed them before. My last name began with an A, so I always sat in front of the classroom. I didn't know I couldn't see well. Anyway, we also didn't have much money when I was a kid, so whatever glasses I had at the time had to last until they broke or until I needed a new prescription.

When I got to junior high school, looks became very important. I wanted to look like everyone else so that I could blend in. But there was one thing that kept me apart...my ugly glasses. They were the queen of ugly. They were what ugly would wear and call it ugly. They were pointed at the top outside corners and I think they were called "cat eyes", but I just called them ugly, or make that UGLY!

Then I remembered what my mom said was required for me to get new glasses. I knew I didn't need a new prescription because when I wore them, I could see perfectly. Darn! So the other requirement was that they got broken. Hmmm. How might they accidentally get broken? I knew I couldn't just stomp on them, that might be too obvious and Mom wasn't dumb. So I had to get a little more creative.

Our junior high building had an auditorium with a balcony. When you were in the balcony and standing at the front row looking down, the space was equivalent to almost a two story building.

So I went to that balcony and stood at the edge and threw my glasses two stories down so that they would "accidentally" get broken. But much to my amazement, those suckers bounced. So I kept throwing them and they kept bouncing. My arm began to get tired, so I had to accept that Mom had somehow bought me not only ugly glasses but ugly and unbreakable glasses. I had to admit defeat. It was clear that I would not be getting new glasses, but Mom didn't say I had to wear them. So when I wasn't in class, I did not wear those ugly glasses. Unfortunately, there was a negative side to not wearing those glasses. I was, and still am, very nearsighted. So when I was at one end of a hallway at school and someone waved to me from the other end of the hallway, I couldn't see them, and did not return their wave. It didn't take long before I got the reputation for being "stuck up". And I was only trying to fit in.

First Dates

MY FIRST "DATE" was when I was 14. I went to dinner with a boy and his parents and more than 40 years later I can remember every detail. We were poor and he seemed very rich to me. I had never been in such a fancy restaurant. They had dishes and silverware that I didn't know when to use, but I think I did okay by observing others at the table. I was wearing a hand-me-down dress but it was from a family who bought only the best, which I needed to fit in with this family in that restaurant. It was a brown and tan plaid jumper and I wore a brown blouse with it. I am naturally shy and I was as nervous as I had ever been in my life up to that point. The boy's first name was Larry and he had an uncommon last name. Since we went to different schools, we lost touch with one another. Fast forward 40 years.

Jenny, a woman my husband worked with, emailed me information about some local events that she thought I might be interested in. She had also sent this information to several other friends. I just happened to look at the list of email addresses and saw that one of them had the same last name as the boy I had gone out with when I was 14. This person had a different first initial. But what the heck. I was curious enough to ask Jenny if they were related to Larry. Jenny told me it was his wife. I told her my story of my first "date" and she asked if she could pass along the story to his wife to see if Larry even remembered anything about it. Neither of us expected much of a response. After all, he was male and 14 years old, and we doubted it made any kind of impression. So Jenny passed on the information and the response was very surprising. Larry remembered every detail of our "date" and remembered the address where I grew up. He remembered my middle name and details about my family. I was speechless and very surprised. It felt really good that even at 14 I made a positive impression on someone.

Typing Class

I'M SURE THAT everyone who attended high school had one class (at least one class) that they especially didn't care for. Maybe it was math for those folks who are "numbers challenged." Maybe it was chemistry class. When would any of us need what we learned in chemistry class?

For me, it was typing class. It was boring and I just couldn't understand why the letters weren't in alphabetic order. Who decided that QWERTYUIOP{} in a row made sense? Can anyone explain that to me? I had to be able to type 60 words per minute to get an A in the class. And I liked getting A's. But 60 words per minute sounded an awful lot like 60 miles per hour, which I know is pretty darn fast on the road.

But I had a special teacher (I believe her name was Mrs. Hensley) who was very patient with me and she seemed to want to help me succeed. I just wanted to survive the class. It should have been an easy class, and maybe it was for everyone else in the class, but for some reason, I struggled with typing. But in the end, I did get my A. Now fast forward to adulthood.

I was raised by my mother who had never really worked much outside the home. This was in the 1960's when moms stayed home and the dad supported the family. But my dad left and Mom became the breadwinner of the house for 3 fairly young children. I was the oldest. We really never felt poor because she found a way to get us everything we needed. Maybe we didn't get everything we wanted, but what we needed was always there. Anyway, I knew that only rich kids went to college, so I would have to find some sort of menial job to support myself.

I can remember looking through the local newspaper's classifieds and every single job that sounded like something I could do required a minimum typing speed of 60 words per minute. That Mrs. Hensley was awfully smart to make me work harder. Anytime I needed a new job, it was always my typing skills that got me the best jobs. Did I mention I now type about 90 words per minute?

Several years ago I had lost my job and was applying with an employment service because I was told they knew about all of the best jobs. So I went to their office and completed the paperwork. Next came the typing test. I was put in a room by myself, but the testers weren't far away. I knew they weren't far away because I could hear them making noise. I couldn't tell if they were whispering or giggling softly. When the bell rang to tell me the test was over, the two testers came into my view and they both had an odd expression on their face. And almost in unison, they said "it sounded like you were hurting the keys." My words per minute that day was 103.

After seeing that kind of result, these fine ladies tried to encourage me to enter a local typing competition. I am basically a shy person and just knew there were too many other people who could type much faster than me and I didn't want to look foolish. Although, when they told me the first price was a Caribbean cruise, I gave it some thought. But the fear of looking foolish beat the slim possibility that I could win a vacation. Later that week, the results of that competition appeared in the local newspaper. And the winning speed was 92 words per minute.

Teenage Driver

I WAS 16 and a new driver when I borrowed my mom's VW Beetle, which had a manual transmission, to do a school project. I needed to collect a variety of leaves and identify them for a biology class. So my friends and I went to an area nearby that was wooded so it would offer a fairly large variety of leaves. It was a beautiful sunny day but it had rained the night before which left all of the plants wet. So every time we walked a little, our shoes and the bottom of our pants would get wet.

After we collected our leaves, we all got in the car to head home. I decided to do the right thing and fill the car with gas. After all, if I did the right thing, maybe my mom would keep letting me use the car.

There was a gas station on the way home that was a convenient place to stop. I must have pulled into the gas station's parking lot at an odd angle, because I found myself heading for the gas pumps. Well, not really the gas pumps, but a shelf that was between two tanks which held motor oil. But I felt confident I could back up, straighten the car, and get beside the gas pump like I wanted. So I put my foot, my wet foot, on the clutch and was about to change gears when the car lunged forward and hit that shelf holding the oil. I was afraid to get out and look, thinking of how much trouble I could be in if I damaged the car. I could imagine never being allowed to drive until I was grown up and on my own. Could Mom ground me until then?

I got brave and stepped out of the car to find that I had done a small amount of damage. I put a dent in the shelf and broke the headlight on Mom's car. I was scared to tell Mom. But the young man who was working at the gas station was being very understanding and even said I could come back after hours to work out some kind of deal, so that neither of us would get into trouble. I was thrilled he was going to help me.

So I drove home not quite as afraid as I had been. But when I told Mom about meeting the guy after hours, she became angry, not at me, but at the guy at the gas station. She told me that she would meet with him after hours to see what kind of deal he was offering. She actually drove to the gas station but would not let me go along. I didn't understand what was happening at the time, but I never heard any more about the incident. And Mom was understanding that what happened was an accident. As I got older and less naïve, it all started to make sense what the deal was about.

Goofy Driver

WHEN I WAS 18 I bought myself a fun 2-seater convertible Triumph Spitfire. Those of you under 50 probably have never heard of a Triumph Spitfire. It is an English sports car and mine was powder blue. It was my treat to myself. I had worked and saved my money and absolutely loved this car and drove it just to be driving it, sometimes with no real destination in mind. I was out cruising with my boyfriend in the passenger seat one day and we encountered a goofy driver. We were in the downtown area of a small community near where I lived. There was a stop light at every intersection of this little town. When I stopped at a red light, I looked in my rear view mirror and noticed a car being driven by a guy that looked just a little older than me. As he approached my stopped car (red light) he hit the brakes late and squealed to a stop, not more than a foot away from my back bumper. The light changed and I drove another block where I stopped at a second red light. This time the driver stopped about 4 car lengths behind me and I'm thinking he was paying closer attention. Before the light changed to green, he hit the accelerator again and just barely stopped in time to not hit me.

I was not liking this game he was playing, and turned left at a red light just to get away from him, thinking surely he would not follow us, but then he followed me through that red light and plowed into the back end of my car. My boyfriend and I got out of the car to check for damage. Luckily, there was only a very minor scratch. The driver of the car also got out to check on things, and that is when we realized he was either drunk or stoned or both. He started begging us not to call the police (for obvious reasons) and told us that he was driving without a license and had taken his friend's car without permission. We knew he would probably take off if we went somewhere to call the police (this was in the dark ages before cell phones), so we led him to believe we were not going to call the police. We drove away and looked back and he was sitting in the grass covering his face with his hands. We did find a phone pretty quickly and called the police and gave them his description, the car's license plate numbers, and the guy's location. I have a feeling he didn't drive anywhere for a long, long time.

Learning Self-Reliance

Richmond Snow

IT IS INTERESTING to me to see how regional some things are and how people see things so differently based on where they live. It can include food, weather, or music just to name a few. In this case, I will be telling a weather story.

I'm from Dayton, Ohio where we get a little bit of many different weather scenarios. It isn't unusual to hear someone say, "In Dayton, if you don't like the weather, wait a few minutes and it will change." I'm sure that isn't unique to Dayton, but does give a good summation of our weather. We can have tornadoes, be affected by hurricanes, and experience small earthquakes. We can experience drastic extremes of temperatures. On Christmas day, it could be 70 degrees or 15 degrees with 6" of snow. In general, living here can prepare you for extremes.

Many people live where they may not be familiar with such weather extremes. For instance, we'll be learning about Richmond, Virginia. My aunt and uncle were living there and I had the chance to visit. We were almost there when it started to snow. The snow wasn't even pretty. You know, the kind of pretty snow that makes it seem like you are in the middle of a snow globe. No, what was happening in Richmond that day was a mix of rain, sleet, and snow. It made the roads very slick. As we drove on the highway, we watched as car after car either spun around in circles or slid off the road. Coming from Ohio, we knew how to handle driving under these conditions. The shoulder of the road was mostly gravel, which could provide a little more traction than the paved highway. We moved the car to our right and drove so that the passenger side tires were in the gravel. This gave us more traction. The local residents must have noticed our car's license plate was from Ohio and assumed we had some experience with this kind of weather. Because when we looked behind us, there was a line of cars following our way of driving, with the right tires on the gravel. That day we had a small taste of how the Pied Piper must have felt.

Oh, and when we relaxed a little and looked around we saw people standing in their yards looking up. It was funny to see those folks see snow for the first time.

Car Mechanic

I **WAS SINGLE** a long time (14 years) and had learned a lot of things out of necessity and lack of money. I had done my own home repairs that included plumbing and electrical problems. I had spackled walls, replaced screens, put down vinyl flooring, and painted every room, just to mention a few things. I worked on my own car as well. To be completely honest, I was lucky enough to have a friend who was a mechanic. I could call him and tell him what my car was doing and he would tell me what needed replacing. Then it was simply a matter of buying the part, taking out the old part, and putting in the new one. Usually.

But there are small details that are sometimes missed by the inexperienced (me). Like when I replaced a radiator in my 1975 Monte Carlo. I had replaced the old one because it had gotten old and had holes that leaked. But for some reason, the new radiator also leaked. It was much less of a leak, but still a leak. At this time, you could go to a gas station and you would find a mechanic.

So I drove to a nearby station and explained to the mechanic that I appeared to have a leaking radiator. He opened the hood to take a look and when he found the source of the problem, he said something like "whatever idiot put the radiator in didn't get the clamp in the right place." I told him I was the idiot. He stammered and stuttered and fixed it free of charge. Someone else might have been offended but I found it very funny, too funny to worry about being called an idiot.

Fast forward several years to when I drove a Honda Accord. I was a single homeowner, worked full time and was attending a community college several nights a week. Free time was a rare treat to me. So when one of my headlights went out, I immediately bought a new one which I had in the car but I had not gotten the time to install it.

One evening I was driving from the college to home and it had been a very long day. I was really looking forward to becoming one with my bed. But that wish got postponed a little. I was maybe two miles from home when my second headlight went out! Yes, both headlights were not working on my very dark blue car, and I was approaching a police station, all the way hoping I could pass unnoticed. But that didn't happen. As soon as I passed, an officer pulled me over, probably thinking I was drunk, so drunk I didn't know I had no lights. Thankfully I had enough evidence to back up my story. I had college text books and one new headlight in the back seat. I also pointed out that there would be street lights all the way home, so he simply followed me to make sure I got home safely.

I Live in Poverty?

THERE WAS A time when my house needed repairs that I just couldn't afford. Some of the items were significant, like a new roof, new windows, insulation, etc. I read in the local newspaper that the suburb I lived in was offering low interest loans to residents who were in need of repairs and met certain low income requirements. It was like a god-send. So I went to the city building and filled out all of the applications for a loan. And I'm crossing my fingers that I get a loan.

It was finally time for me to talk to a loan officer. He looked at my application and asked a few questions. Then he got real quiet, which made me real nervous. I looked at his face, hoping it would tell me something, but his face was very quiet. When he finally spoke, I could tell he had been trying to figure out how to say what he had to say. I don't remember his exact words, but they were something like, "honey, you are below the poverty level, so we will give you the money for repairs and you won't have to repay it." I was stunned for two reasons. First, they were going to give me a big bunch of money to fix my house, and second, I was below the poverty level. I knew I usually didn't have much money, but I was stunned when I was told I was below the poverty level.

Bicycle Hit & Run

WHEN I WAS 30 something I worked for an account-
ing firm in downtown Dayton, Ohio. Every Friday at the
Courthouse Square there was a local band playing and
there was food and beer that could be purchased. The
event was free, and when the weather was good, it
was a great place to be on a Friday evening after work.
On one particular Friday, while I was still at work, I told
a friend of mine that I had a strange feeling that something bad was going to happen to me that night. She
just gave me a look that said, "you are my friend, but
you are nuts." I shook it off and went anyway.

The event had a good turnout. I met a guy, Mike,
and was talking with him for a while. When I decided it
was time to go home, he offered to walk me to my car,
which was probably a good thing, given that it was late
and I was downtown where the crime rate is higher. So
I accepted his offer.

We started walking to my car when a man on a
bicycle came out of nowhere and ran into me and

kept going after knocking me to the sidewalk. I was a bit stunned and bleeding from somewhere above my neck. After I could move without the sidewalk spinning, I got up and took inventory of where I was hurt. My pants had been ripped from crotch to knee and through the rip, I could see that a bruise was forming. And Mike determined that the blood was coming from the top of my ear. He kept trying to get me to let him take me to the hospital, but I'm stubborn and told him I would be fine. I did let him drive me home since I was still a bit stunned. And the man on the bicycle didn't even try to stop, as if someone was chasing him.

When we got to my house, he helped me clean up the blood and bandage my ear. After the blood was removed, he could see that there was a tear in the thinner part of my ear. After he got me settled in, he left. The next morning, I could see that the bruise had grown tremendously. It now covered the whole area of my inner thigh. I don't think I've ever seen a bruise quite that large or quite that color. It was a rainbow of colors that included red, black, purple, green, and yellow. And it throbbed.

When I got to work, I told that same friend what had happened. I think she believed I was making it all up, then I showed her the bruise. She didn't say anything at first, just had her mouth hanging open. Then she said "I'll believe your intuition from now on." It is the only hit and run on a bicycle that I have ever heard about!

Is Love Worth It?

Peeping Tom

I'VE NEVER BEEN a violent person but something happened when I was about 25 years old that made me imagine that I could become very violent. I had thoughts of pummeling another person, and here's why.

I was newly divorced, living on my own, in my own little house in a nice little neighborhood. I felt safe and had wonderful neighbors who looked out for me. It was winter in Dayton, Ohio, which meant there could be snow on the ground.

One evening I came home from work and stayed in all evening. There had been no snow on the ground when I got home, but it snowed some overnight and I was surprised by a little less than an inch of snow, but enough to get my attention. As I was walking on my little walkway to my driveway, I noticed some footprints in the snow. These footprints had started at the street, came up my driveway, went between shrubs that I had close to the front of the house, and stopped outside one of my bedroom windows. I was shocked, confused, disturbed, and concerned. There were also cigarette butts which, in my mind, meant that this person stood there for quite some time if they could smoke more than one cigarette. The confusing part for me was the fact that I had blinds on my bedroom windows that stayed closed all the time. So, anyone standing there could not see in. What were they doing? Did I really want to know?

This happened several times over a period of a month. I felt like a prisoner in my own home. I was afraid to leave, I was afraid to come home. If this person was brazen enough to stand there and leave footprints in the snow, what else was he capable of?

Now comes the violent part of the story. Any time I had to come or go from my house, I imagined myself jumping on the back of this pervert and pummeling every part of him I could reach. Everyone should be able to feel safe in their own home.

Secret Admirers

I **ALWAYS THOUGHT** it would be really fun to have a secret admirer. It would be so romantic, just like in a movie. I would receive sweet little gifts and cards that would be just what I really liked, proving the giver knew all the ways to make me smile and feel special. He would eventually admit to being my admirer and we would live happily ever after. We would have a wonderful story to tell our grandchildren. That's how it is in movies. This is how it is in real life.

I went through a divorce at age 24. It took me a while to work out some personal demons before I felt comfortable enough to try dating again. But I went on a few dates that were more negative than positive experiences. So at age 30, I decided to concentrate on my job rather than my love life.

At about the time I made this decision, I received a beautiful bunch of roses delivered to me at home. There was a card with the florist's name but no name of the person who ordered them. I called the florist shop to ask them who placed the order and they said that the man asked that they not give me his name. But they did remember what he looked like and gave me enough details that I could guess who it was. I worked with an older man who had said things that made me think he would like to take me out. But since he was married, that would never happen and he had no business sending me flowers.

There was another instance about 5 years later. This time I received an arrangement of beautiful spring flowers delivered to me at work. No name, no card from the florist, no way to help identify who it might be. About 2 weeks later, I received a bunch of brightly colored helium balloons. Again, there was no way to identify who sent them. But I would soon get the answer to that question.

There was a younger man who worked in the Security Department of the office where I worked. He occasionally came by my office to chit chat. During one of these chit chats, he asked me out on a date but I nicely declined. His face got red, his eyes were wide open and his body seemed rigid. It looked like he was about to explode, but then he gathered a little composure, enough to say to me through clinched teeth, "I bought you flowers and balloons so you owe me."

I was stunned and a little frightened, and truly did not know how to respond. What I wanted to do was run, run so fast that he couldn't catch me. But reality hit me hard. However I responded, the fact that we worked together certainly complicated things. I believe I said something like, "I'm sorry you feel that way, but I didn't ask you to send me gifts, and I don't intend on dating you based on your anonymous gifts." And then I waited for his reaction. He simply walked away and it was never again mentioned.

That Voice In Your Head

ESP?

I'M NOT SOMEONE who believes in the occult, or whatever you want to call it. I don't believe people can talk to ghosts or can tell someone's future. But there are things that happen that cannot really be explained. I think what I've experienced could be called a premonition. There are two that I recall.

I had just lost my job and a group of friends from work asked if they could take me to dinner for my birthday. I'm not one to pass up a free meal, so I agreed. About 10 minutes (at 5:12 pm) before I was to leave the house, I got a really odd feeling that I shouldn't leave, that someone I cared for needed help. I called my friend and told her I just couldn't leave yet. She said they would go to the restaurant anyway and I should contact them either way. So I waited.

Then the phone rang. It was the local hospital letting me know my mom had been in a pretty serious car accident and that I should be at the hospital with her. I think I got to the hospital in about half the time it should take.

When I got there, I was told I couldn't go into the Emergency Room to see Mom. Well, I didn't care for that decision, so I went back to check on her. She was banged up with some broken ribs and some cuts, but her first complaint was that her clothes had been cut off. When that was her most important concern, I knew she was okay. Now for the really weird part.

As I was leaving the hospital, a police officer stopped me to discuss the accident. I asked what time the accident happened, he answered 5:12 and I was shocked because that was the exact time I got that weird feeling.

One other time I had a hard to explain experience. Sam was a boy I went to high school with. We were friends but also dated a little bit. The relationship lasted more than a year and during that time, I got close to his mother. When Sam went to college, we tried to stay in touch but it was too hard to maintain this long-distance friendship.

We hadn't seen each other for more than a year when I had a weird dream. I could see my friend, Sam, in this dream. He was with his mom and sister and they were in a hospital crying. When I woke up, I wasn't sure what to do about this dream. I tracked down Sam and called him. I simply said, "What's wrong with your mom?" He asked me why I would ask such a question and I told him about the dream. He simply said "it is lymphoma." After that, we both got quiet and I told him I was there for him if he needed anything, but that was the last conversation I had with Sam.

Element of Surprise

SOMETIMES IN LIFE, if you can use the element of surprise, funny things can happen. First, I'll give you some background. My brother is over 6 feet tall and has always had jobs that required physical strength. I am 5'4" and have mostly had desk jobs. But all of the females in my family are naturally very strong. When I was in my mid-20's, I joined a health spa, mostly to reduce stress in a constructive way. The spa I joined had "trainers" that were well educated and very knowledgeable about setting up an appropriate exercise regimen for each person based on their needs and strengths. Or at least that's what their brochures promised. Well, after telling the "trainer" that I had some lower back problems, he set me up on a program that would avoid doing anything to make my back worse. Or that's what he told me, anyway.

The second time at the spa, while doing the exercises the "trainer" suggested, something in my back popped and I could not stand up. I actually crawled to the locker room, got dressed, and drove myself home, all while feeling very lightheaded. When this situation didn't improve, I drove myself to the emergency room where they admitted me with a suspected ruptured disk that would likely require surgery. Luckily, the surgeon I saw was very conservative and suggested lying flat for 6 weeks and if that didn't fix it, then they would have no choice but to do surgery. Thankfully, I didn't have to have surgery.

When I was able to go to the spa again. I started out by talking to the manager and explaining what happened, and I only asked that my membership be extended for the period of time I was unable to work out because of my back. They must have been afraid I would sue them or something, because they extended the membership twice the time I was off and the manager personally set up my workout program. He had been a "Mr. Universe" and he tried to convince me to become a body builder, which I had no interest in. But I did want to become as strong as I could while still looking like a girl. So, here comes the rest of the story, which will explain my earlier statement about the element of surprise.

We were at a family gathering and the guys were arm wrestling to entertain themselves and show how tough they were. I asked if I could get in on the competition. After they all quit laughing hysterically, my brother said he would arm wrestle me. He had that cocky look of someone who KNOWS they are about to make a fool out of someone, this time he thought he would make me look bad.

Well, the arm wrestling between me and my brother began. He was smiling, as if to say, "I'm taking it easy on you, but soon I'm going to kick your butt." Then he noticed that I wasn't backing down. So he pushed harder and the smile on his face disappeared. And I believe he even began to sweat. He looked like an animal caught in a trap. Should he chew off his arm to save his dignity? What could he do to beat me? He started laughing, but it wasn't a normal happy laugh, more like a nervous laugh with a little hysteria mixed in. I gave it my all and held him for a long time, but he wasn't ready to concede. After holding him for what seemed like hours, I gave up. I don't believe he ever again arm wrestled when I was around.

Paint My Face Red

AT ONE POINT in my life, I worked just 2 miles from home, so I was able to go home for lunch most days. It was my habit to fix my food then read the local newspaper while I ate. In the newspaper on this particular day, there was a list of delinquent tax payers for the county where I lived. I would normally just turn the page without giving the page a second thought. But this day, I must have been bored, because I thought it could be fun to read it just to see if I knew anybody on the list and have a chuckle at their expense.

So I'm reading and reading, because it was a lengthy list, and I'm not finding any familiar names. I get about half way through the alphabet and there is a very familiar name... mine! Yes, my name was on the list there for anyone to see and laugh about. I'm thinking this is about as ironic as any situation could be. How could my name be on this list? My taxes were included in my mortgage. So I quickly called my mortgage company to get this mystery solved. Thankfully, it was just a typo that my mortgage company had made when they reported tax payments and they soon had it cleared up. But I can't help but wonder how many people saw my name and thought I was a deadbeat.

RTA Under Fire

HAVE YOU EVER had something happen to you that seemed unreal, like you were in a movie, not reality?

I had a job in downtown Dayton and was lucky enough to be able to easily use public transportation, aka the bus. It came in handy when I didn't have a car for about 6 weeks. Sometimes I could do shopping on my lunch break, as long as I limited what I bought to what could easily be carried to the bus stop. And during rush hour there was a bus about every 7 or 8 minutes that would take me home. There were friends and family who were concerned about my safety, though, because the crime rate in downtown Dayton was much higher than in the suburbs where I lived. But I had been working downtown for several years and had not encountered any problems, until this one special day.

I had shopped on my lunch break and had bought the limit of items I could reasonably carry to catch the bus. I left my office at 5:00 as usual, and walked outside to the corner across from my bus stop. I had almost reached the crosswalk and the traffic light changed, keeping me from crossing the street to catch the bus. I looked up and saw the #7 bus, my bus, starting to move away from the stop. I mumbled under my breath something like "oh, great, just my luck to miss my bus by seconds and have to wait for the next one". Then it happened.

All of a sudden five Dayton Police cruisers came from every direction and surrounded the bus, bus 7, my bus. The officers got out with guns pointed at the bus, bus 7, my bus. There were rifles, there were pistols. And they were all pointed at that bus, bus 7, my bus. Just a few minutes earlier I had been cursing the traffic light that had changed and kept me from crossing the street. Now I am grateful it did change because no way did I want to be across the street in the middle of possible gunfire. So I stayed on that side of the street, walked two blocks then crossed, thinking that should keep me out of the range of bullets. My shopping bags were very heavy but when it was all over and done, that really wasn't a problem. On the local news, it was reported that a man under the influence of something had hijacked the bus and was holding folks hostage at gunpoint. It was resolved without gunshots and no one was injured. Sounds like a movie, don't you think?

First Impressions

HAVE YOU EVER formed a first impression of someone based mostly on outside appearances only to discover
you were wrong? I was on the other end of such an impression. After I was divorced at age 24, I got a little crazy.
I didn't do much by today's standards, but I look back and
can understand why I could give the wrong impression.

My hair was long and permed, looking like a wild child.
I wore very short shorts and a tank top to mow the yard.
Got the picture? Anyway, I started dating the guy who
lived next door and after dating a while, I met his parents.
By this time, my hair was short and straight and I was
dressed more conservatively. While visiting his parents,
the conversation came around to "so, you live next door
to our son? You should have seen the trampy girl who
lived there before you." Their son and I both knew that
trampy girl was me. And when I looked at him, he was
grinning in an evil sort of way, like he really wanted to tell
his parents. I give him a look that said "don't even think
about it". We laughed about that for a long time.

Am I on TV?

HAVE YOU EVER been in a situation where you feel more like what is happening isn't real, that you are secretly in a TV show or movie? Where everything seems surreal? I have. More than once.

Remember, I was raised in the suburbs of Dayton, Ohio, which I believe is considered part of the Midwest. I had no exposure to big cities except as they were portrayed on TV or in movies. I am basically a small town girl. Now put me in Chicago, huge and scary Chicago, Illinois. I had gone to visit someone who lived in Chicago. Now we are going somewhere that requires that we use the subway, the subway in huge and scary Chicago.

So now I am on the L (el?) and there is a young man (the trickster) performing a con on other riders. He has 3 empty walnut halves and a single green pea. He is coaxing people into his game where they will give him $20. Then he puts the pea under a walnut half and mixes them up quickly. The person who gave him the

$20 will now have to find the pea and he will win his money back and the trickster will have to double his money. The trickster does this a couple of times and he always wins. Well, the folks around him keep seeing people lose their money in a real short time. So the trickster is losing business. That is where I come in.

The trickster has turned in a way that most of the people seated could not see the walnuts from all sides. I was the only one who could see that he had a walnut propped up on the pea so that only I could see where it was. In most cases, this knowledge could win a person some cash. Then he tries to pull me into his con by saying "come on pretty lady, show them how easy it is to find the pea." And I am mortified (being a shy Midwestern girl). I shake my head as fast as I can. And I'm sure I have a look of terror on my face. In my head I'm saying "don't make people look at me, don't make people look at me." I would have been very happy to have the earth just swallow me up at that point. I was VERY happy when we reached our destination.

There was another time I felt like I was in a movie, this time a murder mystery. Do I have your attention now? Dayton and surrounding areas are creating recreation trails from old train beds. They are a great place to ride bicycles, walk, skate, you name it. Some folks even ride horses. Most of these trails are surrounded by farmers' fields, some swamps, some wooded areas, and some quaint small towns. My husband and I would ride from one small town to another which was over 20 miles round trip. We have seen some interesting sights while on that section of the trail, which makes it a favorite. We have seen some birds not commonly seen where we live, such as a scarlet tanager and an indigo bunting. We've seen vultures on the tops of old farm outbuildings, just as the sun is coming up and they spread their wings to warm their feathers for the day. We were very lucky to time such a trip as to see this and get pictures. I digress.

On most of our rides, we stopped at the edge of one of those quaint towns, Morrow, and turned around so as to keep the trip a reasonable number of miles. One weekend, we decided to travel a little further, just to see what was happening in Morrow. Apparently, Morrow was a train station in the days of rail travel and most of the historic buildings are still there. Some have been converted to shops such as an ice cream shop and a bookstore. The street is lined with narrow but tall buildings which are mostly apartments over shops. The area is pretty run down and probably more than half of the buildings were vacant and needed some TLC. We stopped in front of the ice cream shop to stretch our legs and struck up a conversation with other bicyclists. They began riding and we walked a little bit to stretch.

Across the street from where we were walking, we noticed a car parked in front of one of those buildings that looked like someone lived on the upper part of the building. And the passenger door on this car was open. And there was an arm hanging out of it. A right arm, I think. I brought it to my husband's attention and we probably had the same thoughts. Why was the door open? Whose arm was that? Were they alive or dead? We both stood there kind of mesmerized, and kind of puzzled, kind of at a loss as to what we should do. The entire time we had been watching, the arm did not move. I'm afraid we were thinking maybe we knew the answer to the last question. If there was a dead person in that car, it was only right that we call the police. At about that time, the arm moved. I think my husband and I both let out a sigh of relief. But the inquisitive side of me wanted to know the answer to all of those questions. And that sight has visited me a number of times and makes me wonder if we should have investigated further.

Police Scanner

TIMING IS EVERYTHING. I've heard that phrase for a long time but didn't understand until a police scanner was involved. Let's go to the beginning. When I was 30, I got braces on my teeth. But first I had to have 4 teeth removed. The dentist who was going to pull those teeth assured me I would be fine there alone, that I did not need someone to drive me to and from his office. The guy I was dating insisted on going with me. As it turns out, I was glad he did. This guy was in law enforcement and had a police scanner in his car. This fact will soon be important.

He had driven me to the appointment and I am really glad he insisted. Those teeth did not come out easily. I was given 23 shots of Novocain (yes, 23, that is <u>not</u> a typo). The dentist put his knee in the chair for leverage and pulled with all his might. I felt a bit traumatized, to say the least. Afterwards my friend drove me home, put me on the couch and went to get my prescription for pain killers filled. He turned on his

police scanner in his car and he heard one of the officers say there was a car in a ditch and he wanted to
run a plate. The dispatcher answered with my name
and address. My friend told me he was thinking I had
lost my mind and started driving somewhere and
ended up in a ditch. The officer had been told it was
a Ford but I had a Honda. The license plate had mud
on it which made it hard to read. I really wonder what
kind of odds you'd come up with to have that happen.
Timing is everything.

Embarrassing Moments

I NOW TRULY believe the old "what goes around, comes around," at least I believe it if it really means what I think it does. I think it means to be careful who you make fun of because the same thing could happen to you.

I always wondered how any woman could walk around with their dress tucked into their pantyhose while their back side was showing, or at least the panties covering the back side. I no longer have to wonder about such things...I can tell you exactly how it happens from personal experience.

I had just started a new job and was about 3 weeks into it when I overslept. I never like being late to work, but being late any time during the first month of a new job was just too much for me to imagine. So I threw my clothes on and ran out the door. The clothes I threw on included a long flowing kind of dress, the kind of dress that was very comfy because it was so light and breezy. Sometimes that is not a good thing.

So I pull into the office parking lot where about a dozen of my co-workers were getting out of their cars and heading towards the front door. Between the parking lot and the front door were about 10 steps up. When I get through the front door I am greeted by one of the nicest security guards you could imagine. He motioned for me to come over to him, so I did. And he said "honey, I think you better go into the restroom and check your clothes." Thankfully, there was a restroom directly off the lobby that I practically ran to, afraid of what I would see. What I saw was my dress tucked up into my pantyhose. I was mortified. There were people in the parking lot who could have brought it to my attention, but they chose to let me walk around that way. I stayed in the restroom for what seemed like an hour, but was probably only 5 minutes, before I could face anyone. Red faced and all, I thanked the guard for telling me. He pointed out that he had daughters my age and he hoped that if the same thing happened to one of them that someone would tell her. But that isn't the end of the dress.

I worked in downtown Dayton and would walk across the Courthouse Square to multiple places that had good lunches. And no matter the weather anywhere else, it seemed like it stayed very windy crossing the Square. Remember what I said about the dress? Think you know what is going to happen? You are probably right. Somehow the wind picked up my dress and smacked me in the face with it, while surrounded by probably 100 people. Not knowing what else to do, I simply peeled the dress off my face, put it back where it belonged, and kept walking. And when I got home I threw that dress away. I had considered donating it to Goodwill, but I really felt that dress was a dangerous object and I did not want to inflict that kind of pain on anyone.

How Many Trucks?

HAVE YOU EVER seen something or thought you saw something until you looked again and really saw something? Did you follow all that? Anyway, here's the story that goes along with that statement.

At one time, I worked at a business about 15 miles from my house. There really was no short or easy way to get there every day. There was a choice of getting on a highway that was notorious for having crashes and stopped traffic, or stay on the surface roads with about 100 traffic lights. This particular day I chose the surface roads.

I was cruising along with traffic which was moving better than usual. So, I'm a happy girl and singing a happy song because I believe this was the way the rest of my day would go. Don't you think that if your morning starts off well that you are more likely to have a day that continues that trend? Well, I think so.

I must have been a little complacent about the good fortune of having all the cars in front of me moving, because then they stopped suddenly and I was afraid I was about to run into the car in front of me. But, thankfully, I got stopped and all of the people behind me got stopped. I was driving a short car and could not see what was happening in front of me. But we were completely stopped.

So, at this point, we might be moving about one car every 15 minutes (no exaggeration). About 30 minutes into it, I was stopped and decided to check out the problem. I looked to my left and in the median strip, there was a semi sitting there and a small pickup truck was behind it. It looked as though the small pickup truck had run into the back of the semi, but there didn't seem to be much in the way of damage to the vehicles. I looked forward to see if traffic was moving and my brain picked up something I wasn't sure about. So I turned back to the left to look at the semi again and I started to count wheels. There were too many wheels in this picture for only one pickup truck to be involved. That's when I realized there was a pickup truck smashed beyond recognition exactly between the semi's front wheels and back wheels. And then it hit me... no one could have survived. And I got the shivers. That's when I started to believe that sometimes our brains filter out things that the rest of us really don't want to know about anyway.

The Kindness of Strangers

HAVE YOU EVER had a stranger make a gesture of kindness that to them probably seemed inconsequential, but to you had great impact? I've been lucky enough to have it happen more than once.

There was a time when I was young, divorced, and had very little money. I had all the bare essentials but after paying the bills, there was rarely anything left for what I would call a splurge. But I worked in downtown Dayton, Ohio, and on Fridays there would be a flower vendor in front of one of the department stores. I think a bouquet cost maybe $5.00 at the most, but that took a while for me to accumulate. I could buy one bunch of flowers about once a month.

I was in line to buy flowers one Friday evening and stood behind maybe 4 or 5 other people. There was a very handsome man directly in front of me. It got to be his turn to get flowers but he hesitated and in broken English said to me "you buy flowers for you?" I said yes and he replied, "No, I buy". He then purchased 2 bouquets and handed one to me. I'm sure I stood there looking stupid and I'm not sure that I even thanked him because I was stunned. He said something in a language I didn't understand. But my goofy romantic personality imagined all sorts of things that he might have said but in reality he probably just said "goodbye" or "have a great day." The timing of such a kindness couldn't have been more perfect. My life wasn't going as well as I had hoped and I was feeling blue. That is why I had decided to splurge and buy myself flowers. To have a stranger buy them, and ask nothing in return, certainly lifted my spirits.

Another young man made me believe in angels and it didn't cost him any money. I had been single for quite a few years, had a lot of really, really bad dates, and felt unlucky, unloved, and unattractive. I had had an especially crappy day and was near tears as I was driving home from work. I was stopped at a red light and just happened to look over at the car next to me. There was a very good looking young man, probably ten years younger than me, waiting at the light also. To my surprise, he smiled at me then blew me a kiss. Maybe that wouldn't mean much to other folks, but because I was down on my life, it was like I had been given a great gift, one that made me have hope that I would find someone special who would love me and share their life with me. And all because of a stranger who blew me a kiss. I try to keep that in mind when I say or do something that could influence another person.

A Girl in Construction (Before it was Popular)

IT ALL BEGAN in 1988 with my suddenly becoming unemployed, and searching for work more exciting than what I had done for the past 15 years. I came out of high school with basic office skills, which lead to a number of secretarial positions. With each new secretarial position, I gained more experience, more highly developed computer skills, and a variety of office management knowledge. It was what paid the bills, but I dreaded getting out of bed and doing it every day. I had found a position at a senior adult apartment complex that at least offered some variety and the chance to make a difference in people's lives. I imagined staying in that position until retirement, but the company was sold and the new management had a different plan. Their reorganization caused me and two other employees to suddenly become unemployed. And that's where we begin.

I felt very lost, unsure of what would come next. I could take another secretarial position and again dread doing it every day, or I could use this time of unemployment to make a drastic change in my life. I chose the latter. Boy, did I choose the latter.

I was combing the classified ads every week for a job I could get excited about. I had no idea what it would be, but believed that I would recognize it when I saw it. It would be a position that was the opposite of everything else I had ever done. It would make me jump out of bed every morning, ready to face a new challenge. Without a college education, I knew I was probably excluded from the majority of exciting positions advertised. But when you have no job, it is easy to take a chance. What do you really have to lose when you have no paycheck anyway?

Then I found the ad that got my heart beating faster. It said something like "Enjoy the outdoors? Good working with a variety of people? Have above average math skills?" I could honestly answer yes to all of those questions. The ad also said they would train the right people to become construction inspectors. It sure piqued my interest. So I decided to send a resume. It's always good to ask yourself "what's the worst that could happen?" The answer here would be that a big group of men would laugh their heads off about a secretary applying for a position to work in construction. But what would I care? I wouldn't be there to hear it, so what the heck. I mailed my resume. And guess what... they called me for an interview.

It was the strangest interview I had ever experienced. And at that point in my life, I'm sure I had been on over 40 interviews. It wasn't easy to surprise me, but this interview surprised me repeatedly. First of all, the Vice President who did the interviewing used very profane language. He was very crude in his conversation with me. In retrospect, I imagine he was testing me, trying to see if I would shock easily, because that is the type of language I would hear every day on construction sites. At one point, he stated that he was only interviewing me because they needed their equal employment points, and "you being a woman gives us a point, too bad you aren't black and you'd give us two points." I made it clear to him that I had no intention of being a "token" that I would never dream of accepting a position I didn't feel capable of handling. And that if he hired me, and I felt I was failing at the job, I would quit and he would lose that point for equal employment. I knew that I might have blown the interview at that point, but I had personal work ethics I felt strongly about and I wanted to be honest about that. He must have wanted me to stand up to him because he hired me on the spot.

Then there was my first day. I wasn't completely naïve. I knew that I would face a great amount of resistance from just about everyone I encountered. You can't be a woman entering a male dominated field and expect everything to be easy.

There I was, dressed in my hard hat and steel toed boots for the first time, feeling very conspicuous. When I arrived for my first day on the job, my new supervisor explained to me that I would be performing various tasks including concrete slump and air

volume tests, soil compaction tests, roof moisture sur-
veys, core sampling, and Windsor probes. He spoke for
nearly an hour describing these tests in detail. I didn't
understand a thing he was saying, he might as well
have been speaking a foreign language. What made
me think I could to this?

Next, I walked down the hall to a room where the
other inspectors gathered to receive their assign-
ments. I was introduced to the senior inspector who
would be training me for the next two weeks. He was
sitting on a wooden chair, leaning back so far that the
chair's front legs were off the ground. He had his arms
folded across his chest and he did not look thrilled
about having me around for the next couple of weeks.

We were assigned to full inspection duties at a
local hospital's expansion. The 15 minute drive there
seemed like an hour as very little was said. The silence
was stifling, the air was alive with tension. This was not
going to be easy.

We soon arrived at the construction site. I got
out of the truck feeling like I was about to step onto
another planet. I was dressed like everyone else, in my
hard hat and steel toed boots, but I felt like I was in
a costume. The sounds of the equipment around me
were like none I had ever heard. They were deafen-
ing. The energy and activity was at a level that defied
description. Everything was alien to me. With each
passing moment, I realized how far out of my element
I really was.

First came the soil compaction test. My trainer
handed me the Troxler 3801B nuclear gauge, a 15" long

steel rod, a five-pound sledge hammer, and a clipboard with various forms on which I would record my test results. My first task was to use the sledge hammer to pound the rod into the very hard, compacted ground. I couldn't recall having used a sledge hammer before that time. Was I about to make a complete fool of myself? I was determined and I put every bit of my energy into this test. My hands were sweating and my legs felt like rubber. I swung that hammer with all my strength and hoped it would hit its mark. Much to my amazement, I pounded that rod 12" into the ground. I had accomplished the first step without too much trouble. Then I inserted the gauge into the hole and recorded the readings onto the appropriate forms. Next, I had to decide on the makeup of the soil. Was it sand with a trace of silt or sand and gravel or sand and gravel with a trace of clay and silt? I just knew it as dirt. How in the world would a person like me know the difference? My trainer explained it would come with experience.

Next came the concrete tests. The first step was to fill my wheelbarrow with concrete. As I walked towards the truck to fill my wheelbarrow, I wondered where I was going to find the strength to push it back to where the tests would be completed. I looked at that wheelbarrow full of concrete and quickly calculated it would weigh nearly 350 pounds. That was almost three times my body weight! Whatever possessed me to believe I could do this? Well, I had committed myself to this and I would give it no less than everything I had. I grabbed the wheelbarrow's handles, took a deep breath and lifted with all my might. The wheelbarrow began to wobble and I feared dumping a very large amount of concrete right where I stood. I took another deep breath, steadied it and moved slowly forward. The 100 foot walk ahead of me suddenly looked never-ending. I concentrated on keeping my steps even, and my arms strong. I felt like all eyes were on me. It seemed everyone around me was waiting to see me fail. Knowing I was being watched seemed to give me even more determination not to really mess up. I somehow managed to reach my destination without dumping the concrete on me or anyone else. I surprised my trainer by completing the tests. I surprised myself even more.

The rest of the day was more of the same and I was exhausted when it came to an end. It wasn't clear to me whether the day's physical or mental demands had caused the exhaustion. I began to think that maybe I could handle this. With much learning and hard work, I was soon able to work alongside the more experienced inspectors. A whole new and exciting world had opened up to me. While not without more than a few challenging situations. I actually conquered a small part of this male dominated world.

I discovered several things about myself by holding this job. One was that I am able to face a great deal of physical pain and do what is required, without anyone being the wiser. I had several accidents along the way, but one accident in particular comes to mind. I was doing soil compaction tests, which requires that you use a sledge hammer to pound a steel rod into the soil. This rod makes a hole in which you place a radioactive gauge. This rod was placed in a plate of sorts, where you could put your foot to hold down the plate and pound the rod into the ground. This maneuver was a little awkward for all of the inspectors, but especially me because I didn't have the muscle power to swing the hammer with one hand. So I had to stand a little crooked and swing the hammer with both hands. At this point, I'm sure I had done at least 100 of these tests, all without incident. But I guess my luck ran out on this particular day.

I was setting up for the test; everything seemed fine. Then I began swinging the hammer. The rod was hitting a great deal of resistance, probably rocks, so I had to hit it more times than usual and it was going very slowly. It made me more inspired to give it my all. So I kept swinging. Without my realizing it, one of the hits caused the rod to hit a rock and the rod was cocked sideways. The next swing of the hammer completely missed the rod and struck my right shin. It is very difficult to describe exactly how that feels. You know how it feels to run your shin into a table? Multiply that by about 100. Things around me began to turn black. Then I saw flashes of light. I began to feel nauseous. I had to take deep breaths to keep from fainting. But above all, I was too embarrassed to let any of the men around me know what I had done. Embarrassment seems to be a great motivator. So I finished the test, packed up my truck, and began to drive back to the laboratory to check in with my supervisor. Driving was very difficult because the pain was so great that I had to drive with my left leg.

When I got back to the lab I stayed in the truck and held down the horn, hoping a co-worker would come to my aid. No such luck. So I got out of the truck and hopped on one leg until I got inside the building. Once inside, I found the closest chair and quickly sat down, trying to decide what to do next. Keeping my lunch down was a high priority. In less than 5 minutes, my supervisor happened by, looked at my face, and immediately knew something was drastically wrong. The fact that I had lost all color in my face was a good indication to him. I told him what happened. After he quit laughing, he agreed I needed medical attention. The company nurse was called, and she came to see my now colorful and very swollen leg. She didn't rule out the possibility that I had a broken a bone based on the amount of swelling. So one of my co-workers took me to everyone's favorite place, a hospital emergency room. After sitting around for over 3 hours, I was seen and it was decided that I had only badly bruised the bone and that I would recover after two weeks of rest and crutches.

I knew that when the story of my accident passed through the grapevine, I would be the butt of every joke my co-workers could think of. That's what happens when you're the minority. Actually, the teasing was less than expected and I discovered that nearly half of the male inspectors had experienced the same sort of accident, only with less impact. Maybe I had more strength than I realized at the time.

Isn't it funny how we get accustomed to seeing people in a certain setting and when we see them out of that setting, we sometimes don't recognize them? Has that ever happened to you? Since I would be on crutches for a while, I was assigned office duty because of my previous secretarial experience. That was fine with me, it sure beat sitting at home doing nothing. I was working in the executive offices, which required that I dress nicely. So I wore dresses, put on makeup and fixed my hair. Keep in mind my usual position there required a hard hat, blue jeans, t-shirts, and work boots. Several times on my first day of working in the office, I would say hello to my fellow inspectors and got no response from them. At first I thought they were mad at me for some reason. I couldn't recall doing anything to upset them, but you just never know. After being snubbed for about the fifth or sixth time, I needed to know what was going on. So I stood in the hall near where the inspectors were gathered, and asked in a loud voice "what in the world is going on? Why is everyone ignoring me?" Every face in the crowd looked stunned and most of them responded "we didn't know it was you." I never really thought about that. I'm sure I looked like a totally different person. They weren't really used to seeing me look like a girl.

Being the lowest on the seniority totem pole seemed to always get me the worst truck the company owned. You know those trucks. The ones that get repaired every week. The trucks that no one else in the company would dare to drive. The trucks that have so many miles, no one knows for sure how many times the odometer has rolled over. It is impossible to remember all of the times I ended up stranded somewhere because my truck wouldn't run. So I'll just tell you about the most exciting and memorable of the truck problems.

I had been assigned a particular truck, which broke down a number of times, had been worked on each time, and then was assigned to me again. On this particular day, I pleaded with my supervisor to show some mercy on me and not give me that truck again. He assured me that it was running fine and he believed it would be reliable. Well, I soon learned otherwise. I drove this truck to a construction site where they were excavating a large parcel of land for a shopping center. I completed all of my tests for the morning and decided to take a lunch break. So I started the truck to leave, or at least tried to start it. And guess what. The truck wouldn't start. I radioed my supervisor who sent another technician, one who was a lot more mechanically inclined than me, to look at the truck or me. He arrived, looked at the truck, and was baffled as to why it won't start, so he called to have it towed away. In the meantime, my supervisor arranged to have another truck delivered to me. Soon after the first truck was towed away, the second truck was delivered to me. This is all happening in the middle of a construction site, about 40 acres in size with huge excavating equipment running all around me. It was time to begin the afternoon testing. I accomplished my tests and was packing up to leave for the day. But this truck wouldn't start now. I swallowed my frustration and radioed my supervisor again, explaining that I'm now stranded in the exact same spot by the second truck for the day.

He, and everyone else who was in his office at the time, had a good laugh then rescued me yet again. This is when the jokes about me being rough on trucks began. And it was to continue for most of my time as an inspector.

Not long after this, I was on my way to another construction site. I only got about two miles from home when the truck quit running right in the middle of a busy intersection during morning rush hour traffic. I was not a popular person at that point and heard countless car horns and saw many frustrated people unhappy with my truck being stopped where it was. Did they think I stopped it there on purpose? Hardly. Luckily, I was close to a telephone where I once more called my supervisor for help. Again, another technician came to my rescue and got the truck started. So I went about my day, completed my inspections, picked up scaffolding for my assignment the next day, and headed home when my day was finished. I was heading home when the truck began to sputter and choke. I just kept hoping it would at least get me home. I was luckily able to get off of the highway before it completely died again. The most unbelievable part of the story for me was that it broke down at the same intersection where I had had problems earlier that same day. So now I'm stuck in afternoon rush hour traffic this time, the only difference being that I'm headed the opposite direction and at least off the road. I again radioed for help and was told that someone will come and get me so that we can put the scaffolding on another truck. I rarely lose my cool, but this had been quite a day. I threw one heck of a fit. First, I got out of the truck and kicked it several times (glad for those steel toed boots). Second, just picture a woman (5' 4" tall) standing in the back of a truck heaving scaffolding off the truck onto the shoulder of the road. It's truly amazing how much strength a person can find in themselves when angry enough. After emptying the truck of every piece of scaffolding, no small feat for someone my size, I felt much calmer. Until I realized that I had probably just entertained hundreds of commuters passing by. Then I felt terribly embarrassed. The only saving grace was that they were people I would never see again. And at times like this, you just have to laugh at yourself and see the plus side. At least all of those people had a funny story to tell their families.

One other startling moment comes to mind when I think of what those trucks put me through. I was driving one of the many junker trucks to a construction site with a fellow inspector. We had been driving a while and needed gas, so we stopped at the nearest exit. I pulled into a gas station that was full service and asked to have the oil checked while we were there. My co-worker had gone inside to see what kind of snacks he could get from the vending machines. The station employee checked the oil and told me that the truck was low on oil and that I should really put in a quart to be safe. I knew this particular truck was a notorious oil-burner so I agreed to have him add a quart of oil. He started putting in the oil. I could only see a little of what was going on in front of the truck because I was in the driver's seat with the hood up. My view was only what I could see through the small space that allowed the hood to be open, about a 3 to 4 inch space. But what I was about to see certainly got my attention. I glanced through that space to find flames that made it seem like the front of my truck was on fire. You never saw a person run from a truck so fast in your life. My fight-or-flight system certainly kicked in at that moment. And when I looked up and saw the startled look on my co-worker's face, I laughed so hard I about cried. Of course, the laughter only came after I realized I was in no danger of going up in flames. Apparently, a small amount of oil had spilled onto the hot engine, which caused the flames. I was told that I was really never in danger. But that's certainly hard to understand when you're in close proximity of flames and surrounded by gasoline.

It would be an understatement to say that most contractors will go to any length to finish a job. Sometimes it would mean that they would try to cut corners by using substandard materials, which was why there was a need for construction inspectors, and hence job security for me. Most days it was a challenge to try to make sure all parties involved were being honest. Sometimes I would be outright lied to. "I didn't put any extra water in that concrete" was a common refrain after I had seen with my own eyes that water was being added. There were many times I'd overhear workers say something like "hurry up and bury that before the inspector sees us", which is definitely against the rules. Imagine their surprise when I would suddenly appear and catch them in the act. Of course, they always expected to outsmart me at every turn, so I enjoyed those times when I could use the element of surprise to keep them in line. But sometimes I was on the receiving end of the surprise.

One day I was in the middle of a job site where the excavators were having a horrible time. The greatest enemy of any excavator is rain, and boy had they gotten more than their fair share. But they still had a deadline to meet. They had tried everything, but the majority of the soil compaction tests I ran failed due to high moisture. I could tell the foreman was getting very frustrated with me. He even off-handedly offered me a bribe if I would pass his tests. No way was I even tempted. I told him he needed to get creative in fighting the rain. And the word "creative" just doesn't do justice to the technique he came up with.

I was parked in the middle of a 40 acre construction site, sitting in my truck doing paperwork when I heard a strange noise. At first I couldn't identify it. As it got closer, it sounded like a helicopter, but much louder. My curiosity got the better of me so I stuck my head out of the truck window. There was a helicopter about 20 feet above me, just hovering. The construction foreman had rented a helicopter to hover as closely to the ground as possible to help dry out the soil so that his tests would pass. Only with passing tests could the job progress and meet deadlines. And it worked! When I returned to the lab at the end of the day and told my story, none of my co-workers believed me. Can't imagine why!

When I first began working in construction, I felt very conspicuous. I guess most of those feelings came from obviously being the only female around. The hoots and hollers that came from the crowds reinforced that feeling. But after I had gotten some experience, and probably accompanying confidence, I felt like I didn't stand out quite as much. That is, until I was assigned duty at a nuclear facility. This assignment required three inspectors, two males and me. This job was in a building which was a highly classified and nuclear active area, which meant we were escorted by an armed guard at all times. This alone felt pretty strange, but it got stranger a little later in the day when I explained the need to find a ladies room. This should have been a simple request, but now I understand that nothing is simple in government restricted buildings. I had to be escorted by our armed guard, which was still discomforting, but the worst part was that my fellow workers had to go along because the guard wouldn't let us be separated. Boy, I sure regretted drinking coffee that morning, and I skipped the coffee until that assignment was over. Some things just don't need to be shared with your fellow workers, like how many times a person has to go to the bathroom.

Being a woman in a male dominated field, I expected to be challenged. I had no problem admitting that I might not have an answer for someone, but was always able to make a phone call and get the answers from my superiors. I also stated, on several occasions, that if a contractor wasn't happy with my performance, I was perfectly willing to call my supervisor and have them send someone else to finish the job. To me, that's making the customer happy, which must be done no matter what your job may be. There was only one time I lost my cool.

I had been assigned full-time to this project, and had been there at least three months. At this point, there was no problem with the contractor being unhappy with my performance. It was a wild day. There were soil compaction tests on one end of the site, and lots of concrete testing on the other end of the site. I was running around, stretched to my limit, but keeping up with the tasks at hand. There was one foreman, Marty, who always complained if he didn't have my undivided attention, and today he was more vocal than usual with his complaints. He went to his supervisor and complained, who in turn came to me with questions as to why I wasn't keeping up with my testing. I told him that if he wasn't happy with my performance, I could call and have another inspector replace me. He told me it wasn't necessary. Well, Marty kept complaining to his supervisor, so much so that his supervisor came back to me to pass on the complaints. And he didn't just calmly repeat them, he got in my face. This man was well over 6 feet tall and I'm just 5'4". He was practically bent in half with his face only a few inches away from mine screaming "Marty said... Marty said..." I lost it. I stood on my toes, got in his face, and screamed "Fuck Marty. If I'm not doing my job, get someone else." I never heard a construction site get so quiet so suddenly, no small task when surrounded by at least a dozen concrete trucks, a concrete pumper, welders, and various other construction work required on this four story building. I must have stunned every construction worker in the vicinity, because as I looked around, they were looking my way with a great surprised look on their faces. I guess they didn't expect little female me to stand up for myself. They were wrong. Even though I was mad at myself for losing control, it seemed to have a positive impact on my work environment. Never again did anyone get in my face!

I soon learned that there were times I could use being female to my advantage. I was assigned to concrete testing at a truck plant. At this point, I was still a little inexperienced, and hadn't figured out the most logical ways of setting up my work area. I had set up my equipment before I knew where the concrete truck would be delivering his load. Since I had to get my concrete sample directly from the truck, it was important not to set up for testing too far from the truck. Remember, we're talking about moving about 350 pounds of concrete in a wheelbarrow. Anyway, I had my equipment set up, trying to stay out of the way of the construction workers as a courtesy. But I messed up. I had to get the concrete, then move the full wheelbarrow through gravel. Have you ever pushed anything in a wheelbarrow through gravel? It is a definite challenge. I couldn't get the wheelbarrow to move. The foreman was standing nearby with his arms crossed on his chest, having a good laugh at my predicament. My face was getting red from a combination of anger, frustration, and exertion. I tried desperately to think of a way out of this. I walked over to the foreman and politely asked him to help me move the wheelbarrow full of concrete. He kind of snorted and followed me to the wheelbarrow, without a word. He was pulling, I was pushing, and together we got it moved, but not without a lot of effort from both of us. He didn't say a word, so I had no idea what effect this may have had on him. But when I returned for more concrete testing the next week, he greeted me at my truck and made some suggestions on how he could make it easier on me. Amazing! I guess when he realized how difficult it really was, he didn't blame the problems simply on my being a weak little girl.

I think I could have worked as an inspector for 20 years and my supervisor would not have quit trying to figure me out. I would catch him sometimes looking at me with a quizzical look, like he wondered why in the world I would want to do that kind of work. He never came right out and asked me, but that's what I read on his face. Sometimes that would make me want to mess with him, catch him off guard, do the unexpected.

During the winter months, when the cold and snow prevented much construction work from happening, a few people were laid off, and those of us left would be given any kind of miscellaneous task our managers could find. You name it, we did it. We built shelves, replaced toilet paper holders, scrubbed walls, shoveled snow off the sidewalks, and filed paperwork, anything to keep us on the payroll.

One day a small group of us were assigned to shovel snow off the sidewalks around the building. It wasn't something we had to be in a hurry about, we just needed to get it done before the office workers left at 5:00. So we shoveled. Then I got an idea, a way to mess with my boss. I found a few small pebbles and threw them up to the second story window where my boss' office was located. Eventually, I hit my mark and he looked out to see what had made the noise. What he saw made him laugh, not only at that moment, but other days when it came to his mind again. I was on the ground making a snow angel. You know, the kind where you lay in the snow and wave your arms to make the wings, and wave your legs to make the skirt. I would bet a lot of money that no other inspector had ever made him a snow angel.

One thing I can say without reservation is that the construction workers I interacted with were quite entertaining. One day when I knew my work load was going to be light, I took my camera to the job site. I love photography and thought this particular construction site would offer me a chance to get some interesting photographs. I was trying hard not to be obvious about having a camera, but since I seemed to draw attention to myself without even trying, secret photographs were impossible. My goal had been to get some black and white shots of "men at work". I was hoping to catch steel workers in silhouette high overhead at strange angles, that sort of thing. I wanted to capture the essence of construction work. But the men around me had different ideas. I never saw so many hams in all my life. Each one had a special pose they thought made them look like hunks, you know, flexing muscles, lifting heavy objects, that sort of thing. Quite a few of the men even offered to strip for me so that I could see their best parts. Several of them got together and decided to pose for me so that I could make a calendar, each one of them choosing which month they wanted to appear in. That was the first and last time I took my camera to work.

At a certain point, I had some health problems that prevented me from continuing my work as a construction inspector. I was hoping the problems were temporary so I didn't have to leave the company. Fortunately, the company had an opening in their environmental department and I was transferred to that department. New laws had recently been passed which said that if environmental hazards were found on any property, it was the current owner's responsibility to clean it up, even if prior owners had caused the problem. Banks regularly hired our company to make sure there would be no clean up problems down the road, and my new department did those inspections.

This position included a great deal of research, including geological studies, hazardous waste generator lists, plot plans, deed searches, and aerial photographs. The work was done in the office and at various government agencies. It also involved a physical site assessment, where we would actually go to the site and record our findings. Usually, by the time we did the physical assessment, we knew what to expect based on our research of the property.

I had called ahead to have the photos waiting for me, so I just ran into the building and picked them up, not worrying about looking at them until I got to the property. The first thing I noticed about the site was the fact that there was a large industrial-type gate on the property that blocked a road of sorts. Why would there be a gate on a piece of wooded property that was never used for anything? As soon as I parked, I took out the photos and had a look. The photos showed this wooded site had a large clearing in the center and there were various objects in the clearing. Aerial photos don't offer much detail so this puzzled me even more. It was time to get out and walk around and see what those objects were.

I started walking on this road which was more like a path in the woods. It was wide enough for a vehicle and had ruts where trucks had probably been driven, but it was similar to a path because there were wild bushes and trees all around. It might have been a pleasant hike in the woods if I hadn't been a little apprehensive about what I would find in the clearing. I walked for about 20 minutes when I noticed an odor. It was difficult to identify, but had an oil chemical kind of smell. My apprehension grew. I almost felt like I was in a horror movie and something or someone was going to jump out at me. This is sort of what happened.

I was looking from side to side as I walked to see if I could find the source of the smell, so I didn't immediately notice what was coming up ahead of me. I looked up and found much more than I expected. There were industrial sized dumpsters, 55-gallon drums spilling over with liquids, and man-made hills which buried who knows what. But what I noticed most was the lack of vegetation. Grass was burned brown. Nothing at all grew in this circle of debris that must have been the size of a football field. This was not good. I was a little stunned and unsure of what to do next. The best option seemed to be to take pictures and make a lot of notes in my notebook. So I did the best I could to describe this mess.

When I got back to the office and told my boss what I had seen, I'm not sure she believed me. I think she thought I was exaggerating because of my lack of experience. Thankfully I was allowed to take the film to a 60 minute developing service (in the days before digital) and show her the proof. It was so incredible to her that she went out to the site herself to see it in person. With further research, it was discovered that the current property owner had run a trash hauling business but didn't have a permit to haul hazardous waste. So he dumped it all in the woods. Needless to say, he did not sell the land, and was in a heap of trouble with the Environmental Protection Agency.

Off Handed Compliments

WHEN I WAS 17 I worked with a man who one day said to me "I bet you'll be pretty when you get older." How does a person respond to such a statement? I'm sure I just stood there, mouth wide open, scrambling my brain to try and understand whether that was a compliment or a put-down. I'm hoping what he meant, in his own goofy way, was that he thought I would get even prettier when I got older, or I would age well, or at least something nice. On the other hand, what does that say about how I looked when I was 17?

Much later, when I was about 50 years old, I was shopping at a local store when the cashier said to me "I'll bet you were pretty when you were younger, weren't you? Again, how does a person respond to such a statement, especially from a stranger? My response was something like "I don't know."

When I think of both of these statements, the only thing I can take from them is that maybe when I was somewhere between 17 years old and 50 years old, I was pretty, maybe.

Stepping on Squishy Stuff

WHEN I BOUGHT my first house, it had a nice wooden deck on the back of the house. It was one of the things that attracted me to the house. I had only lived there about two months when I walked out the back door onto the deck. I didn't have on shoes because I wasn't going to be out there long. In hindsight, I really, really wish I had used the few minutes it would have taken to put on shoes. I stepped on something so squishy it made me slip and it took all of my attention and balance to not fall on my butt. When I gained my balance, I looked around to see what had caused the problem and it didn't take long because there were about two dozen of the culprits…slugs! Big, juicy, nasty slugs. I was young and not experienced in the world of slugs and had never seen ones this large. They looked about the size of a large human thumb, only very slimy. I know that folks in some places like Seattle would laugh at me since their slugs can grow to be 7" long. But when I realized what I had stepped on,

I cringed, shuddered, and jumped up and down while shuddering again. I didn't keep the deck. Apparently, the deck was too close to the ground and stayed wet all the time, attracting the slugs. It would have rotted eventually.

Heights

SAM SHOULD HAVE been a salesman. He can be very persuasive. Early in our relationship, he turned me into a Superwoman. I'll give you a little background first.

I am not fond of heights, not even a little. I couldn't even look over a railing in a stairwell if it was more than one flight of stairs down. I painted the exterior of my house and was not happy about getting on a ladder to paint the upper part of the house. I could only paint as far as my hands could reach without stretching, all the while, having a death grip on the ladder with the hand not painting. My hands would sweat so bad that every time I put the brush in the paint, I would have to wipe my hands on my pants for fear of dropping the brush in the grass below because my hands were slippery with sweat. At one point, a friend stopped by and was talking to me while I was at the top of the ladder and I couldn't look down because I would get light headed from fear of heights.

Sam and I worked together for several years before we started dating. I knew two things about him. He loved to crawl in caves and jump off of cliffs (rappelling). We had lunch together and he basically said that if we were going to spend some time together, I would have to choose to try one of them. I didn't think of either one of those activities as something I would like doing. But he was very persuasive. I chose rappelling.

So we went to his favorite place in Kentucky to rappel, camp, and hike. I honestly didn't know if I had the courage to do this. I know that when you are dating someone, you want to do things that make them happy, but risking life and limb seemed a bit extreme. But there I was, promising to give it a good try.

First, we went to an area with an easy and short cliff, about 20 feet, so that he could explain how the equipment worked. The rope could hold so much weight that it wouldn't even know I was there. There was someone at the end of the rope on the ground that could stop me if I lost control. He would be right there to take care of me. So I tried the short cliff and had so much fun, I wanted to do it again. Especially since he double and triple checked my equipment so there would be no mishaps. I went down a couple of times to feel more confident and then we headed to the real challenge.

Getting up those mountains wasn't an easy walk in the park. Some places required grabbing tree roots to pull yourself up a very steep incline. Some places had round sandstone that caused me to get down on all fours because I was afraid of falling to my death. But I wanted to be brave because I promised him I would be. It took me a very long time to get to the top because I had never done this before and I remained cautious. It helped that everyone involved was very patient with me.

Then we got to the top...it was high...it was VERY high...nearly 200 feet to the landing area for rappelling. Imagine...you are way above the trees...very tall trees. And you are with someone who wants you to go over the side sliding down a little bitty rope. It was about then that I wondered which one of us was crazier; him for doing it or him for thinking I would do it. (Hmm looks like he was crazy either way!)

So here I am, not wanting to be anywhere near the edge of this 200 foot cliff. I am hugging a tree, believing that it would keep me safe and maybe even help me have the courage to really do this. While I'm hugging the tree, the guys set up two ropes; one for me and one so Sam can be on a rope next to me to help me do everything the right way and the safe way.

Sam helps me put on my gear and checks it multiple times, and again explains how safe this is if you do it right, so he walks me through it again. I hear "keep your hand on the bars, keep your legs straight, keep the rope on the rope pad, have your butt lower than your feet, if you go too fast, you should jam the bars together, if you go too slow, take one bar off the rope. And above all, don't look down until he says to.

I am now wearing a seat harness and am attached to a rope that will enable me to slide right down it and safely land on the ground, again, that is 200 feet away. I might have been scared out of my mind, but Sam explained the mechanics of it all and assured me that I could do this. And, besides, we hadn't been dating long enough that I had done something so heinous that he wanted me dead!!

I'm watching Sam on the rope next to me and he explains exactly what I should do. He gets me safely over the edge, where it is too late for me to change my mind and want to go back up the rope. Now he tells me to look down. Yikes (that isn't exactly what I said) I was really up there hanging on a rope. I gained just a little bit of speed and actually landed well for my first time. Wow! It was frightening and exhilarating at the same time. I did it a couple more times that day. And at the end of the day, I was feeling pretty good about what I had done. If I could do that, what else might I be capable of? This event was videotaped and the video is one of my most cherished belongings. In the video you can see me standing way back from the edge and holding onto a tree for dear life with a look of terror. But I did it, all 200 feet of it.

We went back quite a few times and I actually rappelled from a cliff even taller, closer to 300 feet. And I tried it face first which was no fun. I tried climbing back up the rope, but that requires a chest harness and it definitely wasn't made for women. There were times we would meet someone who was curious about what we were doing and would watch us but say they had no interest in trying it. I can't count the number of times I was on the ground expecting Sam to be coming over the edge, and I would see that person who had just said "no way could I do that" coming down the rope with a huge grin. Sam helped us over our fears and encouraged us to stretch ourselves and I'm grateful for that.

Snow Rollers

I'M GOING TO try real hard to use my words to paint you a picture of the sight Sam and I beheld. Anyway, here goes.

It was a typical winter day in Dayton, Ohio. There was a little snow, a little ice, and a little sun, and some clouds. We decided since it was a little over freezing outside that we should go hiking. So we dressed warmly and headed to a nearby state park to go on a hike we had done countless times before. But this day was much different.

To get to the trail head we wanted, we needed to drive along a paved road which was a fair distance, and on any other day would not be a problem. But like I said, this day was much different.

We came around a corner and what we saw made us stop and try to get a grip on what we were seeing. Large snowballs, approximately 18 to 20" in diameter, some even bigger, right there in the road. There were at least a dozen at first sight. They were strewn about like giants had been having a snowball fight. But the surrounding area did not show any voids in the snow like you would see when rolling a snowball in your yard to make a snowman.

Who made these giant snowballs and how? We got out of the car because these snowballs were too large to get around in our little station wagon. At first we were the only people in the park, which gave the experience a feeling of being on some planet where everything is eerie. There was another car at one point, but they stayed in their car, trying either to go between the giant snowballs or over them.

We decided to get out of our car, so that we can get a better look. At every turn, we saw more and more giant snowballs. I know if anyone could see us walking amid these snowballs, we probably looked like we had just arrived on a foreign planet and we couldn't quite get our bearings on what was happening around us. I'm sure we both had that look that says "what the _____?" You can fill in the blank yourself.

We didn't do much hiking that day but instead went home to try and sort out what we had just seen. It turns out they are called snow rollers and only happen under very specific atmospheric conditions. According to Wikipedia, the definition of a snow roller is "a rare meteorological phenomenon in which large snowballs are formed naturally as chunks of snow are blown along the ground by the wind, picking up material along the way." All of these conditions are required; a layer of ice to which snow will not stick covered by wet loose snow with a temperature of near melting point of ice. The wind must be strong enough to move the snow but not blow them away, and it must roll downhill. Considering all of that, we're guessing it is extremely rare and we were very lucky to have seen them.

Escalator

I'LL START THIS story with a statement so that you will know me better. I am not a fan of shopping malls, no way, no how. Never have been, never will be. There are a lot of reasons for that hating of malls, but suffice it to say I do hate them. I live about two miles away from a popular mall and have been there for about 15 years and I could probably safely say I had been to that mall about ten times. I'll tell you about one of my last visits.

I had recently had surgery to repair a cervical disk rupture and had basically been a prisoner in my own home for more than a month. Sam was going to the mall to get something at Sears. My doctor had told me I could start getting out of the house but couldn't drive until I got rid of the hard cervical collar. For those of you who have never worn a collar, it keeps your head from turning or looking down, which makes it really interesting when trying to walk.

We had to get on an escalator to go down one level. Since I couldn't see where I was putting my feet, I had a serious grip on Sam. Sam is a big man and I am thankful for that fact. Anyway, we are heading for the escalator which causes me to work up a bit of a sweat. I don't like not being able to see where my feet are going, but I am so happy to be out of my house that I might begin to feel differently about being at a mall. Then something happens that totally changes my mind.

Apparently there was a screw sticking out of the side wall of the escalator about 3" into the space where my lower legs are, but I can't see it because I can't look down. Then the screw catches on my right pants leg and jerks me hard, so hard that if I hadn't been using Sam as an anchor, I would have gone face down on the escalator.

Then I started shaking to accompany the sweating and added some lightheadedness. Sam walked/carried me to the nearest bench and went inside the closest store and asked the clerk to call Security. When the mall security officer got there, he immediately became defensive. I explained that I wasn't asking for anything other than that the escalator get shut down until repaired and that they replace the pants that almost got ripped off of me. This is one of those times when you wish you could look at yourself to see what others must see. He may have seen the cervical collar and assumed I was faking an injury so I could sue them, which was not the case. I only wanted $20 to replace the pants (if I had bought them at the mall, I would have needed more like $40). Anyway, I had many, many, many conversations with various head honchos there and it was 6 months before they sent me a check for $20. At that point, it wasn't about the money, it was the principle.

Surprises – Good And Bad

The Invisible Car

SEVERAL YEARS AGO we had reached a point when it was time to replace my car. I had been driving a 1991 Cavalier Station Wagon. It was bright blue with a red stripe. It had been fun and reliable for many years, but it was now 13 years old and it wasn't aging well. It had begun to rust, well it actually seemed to be disintegrating. There were quite a few holes in the body of this fun car. That bothered me somewhat. But when it started being less than reliable, it had to go. Apparently there was a sensor that had gone bad and it was overheating, which would shut down the car. And it gave no warning…it just quit running. When you considered its age, it just didn't make sense to throw away any money to have it repaired. So we went shopping.

We knew we wanted something reliable and economical. So we bought a silver Toyota Corolla. It was two years old but like new, and new to me. I was excited because it had been almost 18 years since I had bought a car.

So many cars pulled out in front of me, nearly hitting me, I began to think my car was invisible. I had even been run off the road. I told a co-worker I believed I had bought an invisible car. Then something happened that convinced me of that.

I usually go to a nearby park at lunchtime to enjoy nature, to take a walk, to feel some sun on my face. On one particular day, I was heading to the park and had turned on my right turn signal, had slowed, and was about to turn into the park's driveway when someone plowed into the back of my car. The police report said she was going about 40 mph when she hit me. For anyone who has had a similar accident, you may understand my description. It is hard to describe. But it was like my brain had been scrambled. I couldn't make sense of what happened. I remembered getting ready to pull into the park and the next thing I remembered was that my car was sideways in the driveway and partially on the curb. I was nearby watching and confused.

I like to find something positive in a negative situation, and in this situation I learned that there still are good people out in the world who are willing to help a stranger. A young man was leaving the park as the accident happened. He took my arm and led me to the curb and helped me sit down. He put his arm around my shoulder to comfort me and keep me calm. He called the police to report the accident. At one point I noticed he looked at the back of the car then looked at me and he did this several times. Finally, he asked me if he was really seeing what he thought he was seeing. I said yes, that is a temporary tag on the back because I just bought the car two weeks ago. Then we both burst out laughing. I think my laughter was a little bit of hysteria and it was better to laugh than cry. The ambulance came for me before Sam could get there, so I asked the nice young man to give Sam his name and number because I wanted to find a way to thank him. He promised but did not give Sam the information, proof that this young man was truly a Good Samaritan.

Six Degrees of Separation

THE THEORY OF six degrees of separation is: if a person is one step away from each person they know and two steps away from each person who is known by one of the people they know, then everyone is at most six steps away from any other person on earth. My next story seems to fit that scenario.

My mom volunteers with Judy. Mom doesn't know Judy's last name. Judy mentions she has firewood to give away. Mom tells her we could use it. We go to get the wood. Judy's husband, John, comes out to help load the wood. We finish up and go home. Two days later we see John's photo in the local newspaper. I call Mom to look at it. She looks at it right away and tells me John is the doctor who did my stepfather's surgery. Weird, huh?

Unexpected Gift

I CAN'T IMAGINE there is anyone who has not been touched by cancer. I personally have lost several special people in my life to cancer. Maybe it is because I try to see some sort of positive when surrounded by negative, but I do believe cancer, and the reality that someone will soon pass away, forces us to share feelings we might not have shared otherwise.

My uncle was in his early 60's when colon cancer took over his body and he was at a hospice for his final days. He was surrounded by family. We laughed at silly stories where he was the main character. We each told funny stories about him, things that had not been shared before. Like that when I was very young, I carried a picture of him to show my friends because I thought he looked like Elvis. And like that I remember when I was about 12, I was very sick, so sick that I could not climb the 14 steps up to my bedroom. But if my uncle was around, he would carry me up those stairs and it made me feel like a prince had rescued me.

At one point, while he was in the hospice, he said he wanted to talk to me alone. So everyone else left the room and I walked close to his bed so he didn't have to worry about whether I could hear him since his voice had become a little faint. Anyway, he took my hand and said, "You are the most beautiful person I have ever known because you are beautiful inside and outside." Wow! I would have never imagined him feeling that way, let alone hearing him say it. But I imagine he realized it was now or never, so he shared that with me. And it was an amazing gift. When I might start to feel blue, I can hold onto those words and feel better about myself.

Powerful Words

I HAVE LEARNED over the years that words have great power. Words from another person can brighten an otherwise gloomy day. Words can leave emotional scars that never heal. Words can renew your faith in other people. Words can build confidence or break it down. I try my best to let people know how I feel about them because I know how good it can feel to be on the receiving end of such a kindness.

I was working at a retirement center where only the healthy elderly lived. I had gotten to know several of the residents because my office was in the main lobby and I was the "complaint department". One day I walked out into the lobby and there was one of my favorite residents surrounded by about 4 or 5 of her lady friends, who had come to visit and have lunch with her in the dining room. As I walked by, they were all hugging and I simply said "All that hugging looks great. I don't have anyone at home to give me hugs." They insisted I join their circle of hugs, which I did, and loved every minute of the warmth these ladies offered me. The resident had noticed that I said I had no one at home to hug me and that statement bothered her so much that she came down to my office <u>every</u> day to give me a hug because "it isn't healthy to go without hugs."

I had worked there for 3 years and I really loved the place. I had taken on a special project for the owner and was rewarded with a bonus of $1,000 and was told that I was being groomed for an assistant manager's position, which was quite a step up from being an executive secretary. Then the dreaded day when everything changed. My employment there was terminated without much explanation, only that there were "management conflicts" which I will never understand. Management watched me pack up my personal things and escorted me out the door. I believe I was in shock, physical shock and emotional shock. I had thought that I would be promoted and work there until I retired. That was not in management's plan.

It took me a good month to be able to even think about walking into that building again, but I wanted the chance to say goodbye to the residents I had become close to. I called one of them and asked if she could let a few of my favorite residents know that I planned to visit that evening after the staff had gone home. That's when I discovered that the residents were upset with me because they were told by the General Manager that I quit without notice. And they were hurt that I hadn't said goodbye. I told them that I would explain when I got there.

When I got there they looked like puppies who had been beaten and I knew that what they had been told had made them very unhappy. But when I told them I had been asked to leave, their expressions changed to some pretty fierce looking anger. They wanted to take action and right this wrong. I couldn't imagine what they could do to change the situation but the fact that they wanted to take action made me feel their caring. I got my hugs and went home and, of course, cried for hours because I would not be a part of their lives anymore. About a week later, one of the ladies called me at home to let me know they had circulated a petition to help me get my job back and that over 100 people had signed it. They planned to give it to the general manager the next day and would let me know if the petition worked in getting me back. I let them know how much their gesture meant to me, but I really doubted that the decision would be reversed. But what a giant hug that was!

Anyone Can Be an Angel

RECENTLY, I WAS reminded that anyone can be an angel. Almost 10 years ago, I worked with a man named George who had daughters my age, so he was like a father figure. He was just an all-around nice and interesting person. We had worked together for almost a year when he was let go. As the manager of Human Resources escorted him out, I said "I'll miss you George. I really enjoyed working with you." It was a simple heartfelt response to watching him leave. I truly meant what I said so I didn't give it another thought.

About 5 years passed and I happened to see him again. He hugged me and told me how much he appreciated what I had said, that no one else at the company had even talked to him. I had no idea that what I said at the spur of the moment had such an impact. We really have to choose our words carefully.

Part 2

Laugh Or Cry
(Your Choice)

What Is Parkinson's Disease?

PARKINSON'S DISEASE (PD) is a chronic and progressive brain disorder, which means that symptoms continue and worsen over time. Nearly one million people in the US are living with PD, which is more than ALS, Muscular Dystrophy, and Multiple Sclerosis combined. The cause of PD is unknown and there is no cure. There are, however, treatments that can reduce the symptoms.

Typical symptoms include:

- tremor of the hands, arms, legs, jaw, and face
- bradykinesia or slowness of movement
- rigidity or stiffness of the limbs and trunk
- impaired balance and coordination
- depression

Other less common symptoms can also include:

- the loss of the sense of smell
- your handwriting becoming small
- the inability to make facial expressions
- not swinging your arm when you walk
- your voice becoming softer and others may not hear you
- having difficulty focusing on one task at a time

These symptoms vary from person to person. The tremor can affect only one side of the body but may progress to affect both sides. No two patients experience identical symptoms.

My Experience with Parkinson's Disease

MY STORY STARTS in 1998 when I was in my early 40's and kind of a newlywed, married 3 years at that point. We enjoyed a lot of the same things such as hiking and camping, and as you've read earlier, my husband convinced me to try rappelling and caving. To get to the point, we enjoyed being active and outside. Then I was diagnosed with Parkinson's Disease (PD) and my life would never be the same.

The average age at diagnosis of PD is 65. Saying I was surprised with the diagnosis at 42 years old is certainly an understatement. But I've had multiple health issues since I was very young. The most important thing I've learned with all of these ailments is that you have to keep your sense of humor if you are going to survive. Parkinson's is no exception. I've given you a list of the most common symptoms of the disease, but there are some odd symptoms as well. Because it causes stiffness in your joints, you have a greater chance of falling, and the PD takes away the ability to right yourself. Some of the goofier symptoms of Parkinson's need a little explanation and include:

Getting Stuck: If I'm in a crowd and someone stops me, it is difficult to get moving again. To get moving again, I take an exaggerated step, like I'm stepping over something in my path. Sometimes, when I am out with friends, it is helpful for someone to take my hand and pull me through the crowd. There was also a time when I had trouble walking, but I could run normally.

Regulating Body Temperature: If it gets above 72 degrees or so, I am very uncomfortable and my whole body sweats. I sweat so badly that my clothes and hair become soaked. Sweat runs into my eyes. Once I get this hot, it can take hours to cool off. I'm hesitant to go anywhere because of the embarrassment of walking around in sweat soaked clothes.

Sleep Disturbances: Most resources list "sleep disturbances" as a possible symptom, but I have never found a specific definition for this. I can tell you about my sleep disturbances. I rarely get more than 5 hours of sleep a night. Typically, I have trouble getting to sleep. I've tried severely limiting my fluid intake after 6:00 pm. I exercise as early as possible in the evenings so as not to affect my sleep. I sometimes take a Jacuzzi bath to relax. I will have a glass of wine occasionally. Nothing seems to help. I eventually reach total exhaustion and will sleep 8 or 9 hours which seems to catch me up for a little while. Then the cycle begins again. Another "sleep disturbance" is that I have begun having very vivid dreams. Recently I had a very frightening dream. I had fallen asleep on the couch. I dreamed someone had broken into my house and was trying to drag me out of my house. When I woke up, I was screaming and flailing my arms and kicking an imaginary intruder. I did not get back to sleep after that. I don't recall ever having such realistic dreams before PD.

Muscle Cramps: Before PD, I had occasional muscle cramps that I believe were caused by overuse. You know the kind, the foot cramp that makes your toes go in different directions. That kind of cramp generally is pretty painful but goes away fairly quickly. Muscle cramps relating to PD falls into a completely different category. Not only are they much more painful, they also occur in unusual muscles and do not stop quickly. It would be difficult to say which muscle hurts the most. The top 5 would include the forearm, hands, ribs, thighs, and that muscle located sort of under the arm but a little farther back.

There are questions my doctor asks just about every time I see her that make me believe there are other symptoms to come such as' Can you roll over in bed? Can you get in and out of a car easily? Have you had any hallucinations? Have you had any incontinence? Because brain chemicals are involved, it is difficult to know if I'm experiencing PD symptoms or side effects from the medications. It's a balancing act that my doctor handles well.

There isn't a definite time when the Parkinson's Disease (PD) became a problem. It is a disease that is sneaky, it gradually takes away your ability to live normally. My PD story started when the index finger on my left hand started to twitch. I remember laughing about it and showing it to friends. I just assumed it was some sort of problem with the nerves in my hand since I typed for a living. Then I started having pain in my hand and the twitch became more intense. But I still wasn't too concerned since I typed 8 hours a day. The pain increased to the point that I couldn't ignore it, so I went to my family doctor.

My family doctor felt like it was most likely carpal tunnel syndrome. In my mind, that was the most likely answer, again, because I typed for a living. I was given a wrist brace for each hand. That was going to be an easy fix so I wasn't worried, at least not until the braces came off and nothing had changed.

The next odd thing I noticed was that I was very clumsy and dropped things regularly. Since I've never been really graceful, I still wasn't worried.

My husband, Sam, and I liked to hike. He usually walked in front of me so that he could be the web catcher. I really, really, really dislike walking into a spider web with my face. So, thankfully, he was my web catcher. We were hiking and for some reason I was walking in front. We had been walking for maybe an hour when my husband asked what was wrong with my left arm. I didn't know what he meant, so I asked for clarification. He said my left arm wasn't swinging when I walked like my right arm did. I had not noticed this. I still wasn't worrying but was curious enough to call my doctor.

The family doctor was a little lost so he sent me to a thoracic surgeon who ran some tests and told me it was probably thoracic outlet syndrome, compression of the nerves or vessels between the neck and armpit, but there was no treatment other than surgery. I said no thanks and kept living my life. Maybe 2 or 3 months later, I noticed that I was dragging my left leg and that if I walked for very long, my left foot would turn in and I walked on the side of my foot, which was painful. Now I'm worried!

I went back to my family doctor who sent me to a neurologist who ordered a series of tests. These tests included a 24 hour urine collection (that was fun), a lumbar puncture (even less fun), EMG, MRI, and lots of blood tests. When the results were gathered, he still didn't offer a diagnosis. At this point, he knew what it wasn't. He was thinking it could be PD but since there is no test for it, he still wasn't ready to say that was it. He sent me to the nearest teaching hospital, Ohio State University (OSU), to see the PD expert. He looked over my test results and decided I should be started on PD medications and if my symptoms got better, it must be PD. So I went back home to the local neurologist for treatment. At this point, it has been almost a year since my finger twitched.

During all of these doctor's appointments, a little voice said there was something wrong with my neck. I had no specific pain or symptoms other than those mentioned, but told each doctor "check my neck". They each ignored me because my symptoms had nothing to do with my neck. Finally, I think my family doctor just got tired of listening to me, so he ordered an MRI of my neck. When the results came back showing a ruptured disk, I was quickly sent to a neurosurgeon who scheduled an immediate surgery because according to him, if I had stumbled just a little, I would have been paralyzed from the neck down. And I had no symptoms! So listen to the voice in your head and don't let it be ignored.

Anyway, after recovering from surgery, I was again forced to deal with the PD. The first neurologist I saw came highly recommended, so I followed his directions, at least for a while. At one of my appointments, I asked a serious question about what my future might hold and for some reason, he found my question humorous. Have you ever had a doctor laugh at you in a way that says "I think you are stupid"? Well, I didn't care much for it. This condition is a life-long issue and I needed to find a doctor who wouldn't laugh when I was serious and scared about my future. So I changed doctors.

This neurologist also came highly recommended. He always had students or interns with him which I was told was a sign of a well-respected physician. When I saw this physician, he would conduct his exam and then dictate while he was still in the room. He dictated that he saw a slight tremor in the right hand, which was wrong. The tremor was only on the left and at times, I used my right hand to control the movement in my left hand. When I explained that to the doctor, he not only laughed at me, but argued with me. That wasn't going to work for me.

I knew I would have to find a doctor who would listen as well as teach me about my condition, so I asked around. A friend has a sister with MS who saw a neurologist she absolutely loved, so I made an appointment. It was a perfect match! I drive almost an hour for my appointments and would drive even further if I had to.

Over the next 10 years or so, my symptoms would change and/or increase in intensity and my medications would be changed. The new symptoms would include falling, which was the most disturbing.

It is really hard to explain how this feature of PD feels. The first time I fell, I was very lucky not to be more seriously hurt. It was a simple move, I only needed to walk down the 3 steps that separated the kitchen from the garage. Somehow, my body leaned to the right and threw itself off the steps, causing me to land between a metal spike and shelf full of poison (lawn chemicals). Soon after I landed, I began taking inventory of my possible injuries. My arm had a significant cut and was causing a puddle of my blood to gather below me. I somehow had become wedged between the metal spike and the concrete steps with my head lower than my body. I felt dazed and confused, and wasn't sure how to get out of that position. I eventually extricated myself and realized I had lots of abrasions and bruises, and was thankful for the minor injuries. I was falling with some frequency. My body would sometimes get ahead of my legs and I would fall forward and couldn't stop it. It was like being a cartoon character whose legs kept trying to catch up with their body. For the most part, these falls injured my pride more than my body. I began having problems walking on any surface that wasn't completely flat and smooth, and I always held on when I was on steps.

One of the most frustrating things about PD is that you cannot predict which symptom is going to appear and when, and there is nothing I can do about it. I consider myself a logical thinker. With some medical conditions, if you pay close attention, you can usually find a cause and effect situation and possibly control the condition. For example, if you realize that your shoulder only hurts when you sleep on that side, then you stop sleeping on that side. There is little you can do yourself that helps in any way...with two exceptions. Exercise and attitude.

I know that exercise helps me minimize my symptoms a bit but even that gets complicated. Since I can fall without warning, I am not always comfortable walking by myself. My sister, who lives too far away to walk with me, sent me a cell phone so that I can at least call for help. I recently moved to a new house and I wanted to get a look at the neighborhood. Some of the sidewalks were tilted from tree roots pushing them up. I went for a walk and thought I was paying extra close attention, but suddenly I found myself on the ground. I fell completely flat on my face. My glasses popped off my head and my face hit the sidewalk. I took a quick inventory to see if I had done any real harm, and since I saw no blood, I stood up as quickly as possible. I had some scrapes and bruises and was thankful I didn't break my nose or worse. What hurt the most was that a man was sitting on his porch and witnessed my fall. That definitely hurt my pride. He yelled across the street to ask if I was okay. When I said yes, he pointed out that I had hit my head and that I should be sure that I was okay. I thanked him and walked home.

A week later I fell while going into a grocery. Two women rushed over to help me. When I said I was okay and that I fall all the time, they looked at me like I was crazy.

Any kind of exercise you can do is helpful so that your body makes more "feel good" brain chemicals. My exercise of choice right now is a recumbent tricycle. It is low to the ground and has 3 wheels so I don't have to worry about having bad balance. I live in Dayton, Ohio, and there is an extensive bike trail system that makes it safer than riding on the streets. When I exercise regularly, I sleep better, my symptoms improve a bit, my mood is better, and I think more clearly. Why would I not exercise regularly when there is so much benefit to it?

Laugh in the Face of Adversity

I **WORKED AS** a medical transcriptionist for a group of four eye surgeons. I had worked in this office for about 12 years at the time. The senior partner, I'll call him Dr. C, and I joked around and were comfortable with each other's weird sense of humor. But Dr. B had recently joined the practice, so he hadn't been exposed to this weird humor.

Anyway, one day I was talking to both doctors and was showing them something on a piece of paper that I held in my left hand, which is where the tremor was. The paper was shaking, almost violently, so I moved it to my right hand. Dr. C looked at me, and with a straight face, said "I'll bet that tremor could come in handy when you want to toss a salad." I found it very funny and began to laugh, then I looked up at Dr. B and he was looking shocked, like a deer in headlights. Then he started to say something and it comes out like uh, uh, uh, and nothing else. I found this even funnier and couldn't help but laugh even harder. The poor man was never able to form words or comment on what had just been said, but simply walked away.

Another odd part of the disease is the inability to maneuver yourself well enough to get your arm in a sleeve. I was having breakfast in a restaurant with my friend Ellen who I had known for probably 30 years at that point. She was that friend that everyone should have. She always makes me laugh and is the most laid back person you could meet. And it isn't that she doesn't care enough to get stressed about bad things, it is just that she has learned the value of not taking everything too seriously. So we've finished eating and our husbands have gone to the bathroom and we were still at the table getting ready to leave. I stood up to put my jacket on and I absolutely can't get my left arm in the sleeve. I asked my friend for help and I made a comment like "that Parkinson's is a funny disease." And her response was "I don't think it would be funny at all." And it wasn't what she said exactly that made me start laughing almost hysterically. It was because I had never really seen her that serious, and for some reason that was funny to me. I don't think she understood what I was laughing about. Maybe she still doesn't even 10 years later.

Early on, soon after I got the diagnosis of Parkinson's Disease, I was encouraged to join a support group. I had joined support groups in the past for other health issues. But this situation seemed different. I was a young patient with different needs than someone in their 70's, like how to keep my job and my health insurance. I was also afraid that I would meet people whose symptoms were much more advanced than mine because I would feel like I was seeing my future. That kind of future scared me quite a bit. With this disease, I feel like taking one day at a time is a better plan. I did call the local Parkinson's support group and the woman who answered the phone said "if you have to have a neurological disease, at least this one won't kill you." At that point, it felt like she had smacked me in the head. But it was definitely something I needed to hear. It always helps to be reminded there are plenty of people with more serious problems.

In the past, when I've met new neighbors, I introduce myself and tell them that if they see me walking funny, it isn't because I'm drunk, it is the PD. What isn't so funny is that I've been told that a friend of a friend, who has PD, was arrested for public intoxication. I've heard other stories that are funny afterwards, but if the public was educated about PD, it would never have happened. I worked for someone whose father had PD. The family was at a public event and they were sitting on bleachers. Well, her father had to go to the restroom, so he got up and worked his way down the row, trying not to trip or step on anyone. At one point, he gets "stuck". This happens to me and it is difficult to explain. It is like your brain quits sending the order for your legs to move, and you just stop and can't get going again. Anyway, when her father gets stuck, she yells at strangers to "push him". Can you imagine someone telling you to push an elderly stranger? Could you do it? After some time, one brave woman gave him a gentle push and he got going again.

I have a friend, Margo, who worked with me at the doctor's office. She has a really goofy sense of humor, which is one of the best things about being her friend. Several of us were talking about how it was nice that our office provided translators for patients who were deaf. I mentioned that I had taken some classes in American Sign Language and that it was something I enjoyed and that it came easy to me. Margo told me that our local community college offered a certificate program in American Sign Language and that I should look into it. I told her I didn't know how effective I could be with the hand tremor and all. She says "that's no big deal, they would just think you stutter." I laughed until I snorted, which got everyone's attention, then Margo starts laughing loudly, tears were running down both of our faces, and we were attracting the attention of anyone within hearing distance.

My Miracle

I **WANT TO** end on as positive a story as possible, so I'll tell you about my miracle. When I was diagnosed with PD, I was given one medication until new symptoms appeared and then was given an additional drug. I was up to 4 drugs at the point when I had been dealing with PD for about 9 years. My symptoms had become fierce. I was falling, I didn't walk right because I dragged my left leg. My balance was greatly affected, so much that I couldn't walk in our back yard without holding onto my husband. I had traveled to South Carolina for a girls' trip and while there, I became intensely aware of my problems, and for the first time I felt handicapped. And I didn't like it, not even a little bit.

At about the same time, I saw my neurologist for my regular visit. While there, she told me about a new medication that was now available. She gave me a low dose of this new medication. Within a couple of weeks, all of my symptoms virtually disappeared. Someone meeting me for the first time would never guess I had PD. And those people who had seen me at my worst were brought to tears when seeing the improvement for the first time. I felt inspired to do something big, really big. I needed a way to celebrate.

I thought about what I would do and came up with a plan/goal. I wanted to go to the Smoky Mountains in Tennessee and hike 25 miles in 5 days. In looking back, I'm not sure why I chose this goal. I had never hiked that much in such a short period of time. And now I was in my 50's and 50 pounds overweight. I'm not sure why I thought I could do this.

I had the goal and realized that maybe I could get sponsors to raise money for PD research. So I asked my family, friends, and co-workers to pledge money per mile and everyone I asked said they had no doubt I could do it. If I did make it the 25 miles, I would raise a little over $600. This wasn't huge money, but I figure every dollar given for research helps them get closer to a cure.

I called my wonderful friend Ellen, whom I had known for more than 35 years, to see if she would have interest in going with me. She said yes without hesitation. So we were off on an adventure, one that I could not have done alone. Ellen was the perfect hiking buddy because she was physically fit, she has a can do positive attitude, and she would push me if I slowed down, but the push would be a gentle one. Thirty-five years before, we were on our first grown up vacation right out of high school right there in the Smoky Mountains. Can you say "meant to be"?

We arrived at the Smoky Mountains Park Visitor Center to get maps and choose our trails for the week. We knew that ultimately we needed to average 5 miles a day to reach our goal. We also realized the weather could play a part in our success. One day we hiked in the pouring rain, and not a nice warm summer rain, but a cold April rain that chilled us to the bone. But we got our 5 miles for that day. The third day we hiked several different trails because we were feeling great and the weather was beautiful. We were close to the end of our hiking for that day when Ellen asked me if I realized how far we had gone that day. I honestly didn't know. I had just kept putting one foot in front of the other. We had hiked over 9 miles!! I burst into tears, I think because I was so overwhelmed by what we had done and I was feeling completely exhausted. We began to add up our miles for the week and realized we only needed 4 more miles and we could go home a day early. WOW! I don't remember having any pain and I slept like the dead.

We met a lot of nice people along the way and when Ellen told them why we were there, they were very supportive. We even got a free meal at the restaurant next to our hotel. The manager said our story was the most inspirational thing he had ever heard and paid for our dinners. The most inspirational story? Something I did? An overweight middle aged woman?

While we enjoyed our free meal, we were talking to the manager about our goals and he asked what organization put this trip together. I answered "I just made it up". He got a really odd look on his face, and Ellen started laughing, I was lost as to what had brought that about. Then I stopped to think about what had just been said. While my answer was meant to explain that I was doing this walk because it was something I wanted to do personally, what the manager heard was that I had just lied to him to get a free meal. Now I got it!

Not only did we reach our goal, we actually hiked 25.6 miles in 4 days, and had fun doing it. This trip taught me several things. I am capable of doing difficult things when it is important to me. And I am very fortunate to have such a good friend as Ellen.

A month later, Sam and I went to the Smoky Mountains and hiked 16 miles, including one trail that was a significant challenge for me. It reminded me to slow down and pay attention to what I was doing so I wouldn't trip and fall. And I made it without mishap.

Attitude & Why?

I **STRONGLY BELIEVE** that a person's attitude or outlook can seriously impact what direction their life takes. If we choose to believe in a positive outcome, we are more likely to get a positive outcome.

I also believe that we have all had hardships in our lives that we didn't cause ourselves. For some it could be health problems, or loss of a job through no fault of their own. At some point, we ask "why me?" Research regarding PD points to two possible causes of the disease, heredity and chemical exposure, neither of which is a factor in my case. There is no known family history and I have not worked in a job that exposed me to serious chemicals.

I believe that situations like my having PD happen because God has chosen me for a special purpose. And I believe it is my duty to educate people about PD. When strangers see that something is "wrong" with me, I try to put them at ease by telling them I have Parkinson's Disease and then ask if they know anything about it. A high percentage of the time their answer is "no". Then I ask if they want to know about it. About the same percentage say "yes", so I give them the basics. And I try to use humor because that along with a positive attitude are the best weapons we have to overcome any kind of adversity. According to the Parkinson's Disease Foundation, one million people suffer with Parkinson's and there will be 60,000 newly diagnosed cases this year, many of those will be under 50 years old. It looks like I have a lot of people to reach. You can help by sharing what you've learned by reading my book. Thank you.

32290733R00092

Made in the USA
Charleston, SC
14 August 2014